WEAPON

THE 'BROOMHANDLE' MAUSER

JONATHAN FERGUSON

Series Editor Martin Pegler

OSPREY PUBLISHING
Bloomsbury Publishing Plc

Kemp House, Chawley Park, Oxford OX2 9PH, UK
29 Earlsfort Terrace, Dublin 2, Ireland
1385 Broadway, 5th Floor, New York, NY 10018, USA
Email: info@ospreypublishing.com
www.ospreypublishing.com

OSPREY is a trademark of Osprey Publishing Ltd

First published in Great Britain in 2017

A catalogue record for this book is available from the
British Library.

Print ISBN: 978 1 4728 1615 3
ePub: 978 1 4728 1617 7
ePDF: 978 1 4728 1616 0
XML: 978 1 4728 2343 4

Index by Rob Munro
Typeset in Sabon and Univers
Page layouts by PDQ Digital Media Solutions, Bungay, UK
Printed and bound in India by Replika Press Private Ltd.

24 25 26 27 28   12 11 10 9 8 7

The Woodland Trust
Osprey Publishing supports the Woodland Trust, the UK's
leading woodland conservation charity.

www.ospreypublishing.com
To find out more about our authors and books visit our
website. Here you will find extracts, author interviews,
details of forthcoming events and the option to sign-up
for our newsletter.

Dedication
To my wife Helen, for her support and especially her patience!

Acknowledgements
In the process of researching and writing this book I have
received invaluable assistance from many people, including
specialists and collectors who have forgotten more about the
'Broomhandle' than I will ever know. These people have also
readily supplied images, many of which have not previously been
published. I would like to thank in particular Dr Geoffrey
Sturgess (to whom special thanks for his efforts in fact-checking),
King Rhoton, Dr Leonardo Antaris, David Witkowski, Richard
Milner, Leroy Thompson, Kenneth Smith-Christmas, Lar Joye of
the National Museum of Ireland, Lin Xu, Gerben van Vlimmeren,
Mauro Baudino and Philip Jowett, as well as Jacob Bishop, Chris
Streek, Mike Sterry and my other Royal Armouries colleagues.

For quotes reproduced from the speeches, works and writings of
Winston S. Churchill:
Reproduced with permission of Curtis Brown, London on behalf
of The Estate of Winston S. Churchill.
© The Estate of Winston S. Churchill.

Artist's note
Readers may care to note that the original paintings from which
the colour plates in this book were prepared are available for
private sale. All reproduction copyright whatsoever is retained by
the Publishers. All enquiries should be addressed to:

Peter Dennis, 'Fieldhead', The Park, Mansfield,
Nottinghamshire NG18 2AT, UK
Email magie.h@ntlworld.com

The Publishers regret that they can enter into no correspondence
upon this matter.

The Royal Armouries
The Royal Armouries is Britain's national museum of arms and
armour, and one of the most important museums of its type in
the world. Its origins lie in the Middle Ages, and at its core is the
celebrated collection originating in the nation's working arsenal,
assembled over many centuries at the Tower of London. In the
reign of Elizabeth I, selected items began to be arranged for
display to visitors, making the Royal Armouries heir to one of
the oldest deliberately created visitor attractions in the country.
The collection is now housed and displayed at three sites: the
White Tower at the Tower of London, a purpose-built museum in
Leeds, and Fort Nelson near Portsmouth. To find out more,
explore online at collections.royalarmouries.org

Front cover, above: An early C96, serial number 4528. (© Royal
Armouries PR.11417)
Front cover, below: A well-known image of the M712
Schnellfeuer in Waffen-SS service, 1942. (Tom Laemlein /
Armor Plate Press)
Title-page image: Armenian civilians armed and ready to defend
themselves from Ottoman violence, c.1915. (Courtesy of
David Witkowski)

CONTENTS

INTRODUCTION

Today, on hearing the word 'pistol', we automatically think of self-loading designs produced by companies like Colt and Glock. But in the 1890s, the revolver was absolutely dominant, to the extent that even the word 'revolver' had become synonymous with 'pistol'. Single-shot and multi-barrelled pistols had largely fallen by the wayside, being similar in size, weight and cost to a revolver, but lacking in capacity. At the same time, one of the world's famous gunmaking firms, Waffenfabrik Mauser, sought to enter the lucrative pistol market. Known to most simply as 'Mauser', the present-day company can trace its history back beyond the creation of the German state. In 1811 a state arsenal was founded in Oberndorf by Friedrich I of Württemberg. The factory's landmark design was the bolt-action mechanism conceived by the Mauser brothers Wilhelm and Paul in 1867. Four years later their Gewehr 71 rifle became the first standardized arm of the new German Empire. A series of successful refinements followed, and by the end of the century Mauser had arrived at its definitive bolt-action magazine rifle design. The Mauser Gewehr 98 remains in production after well over a century, and variations on the design are found across a range of civilian and even military precision rifles today.

As a result of this unrivalled success with rifles, Mauser also produced a less well-known series of pistols, beginning in 1877 with the C77 ('C' standing for *Construktion* meaning 'design') single-shot pistol. Their first

The Mauser M1889 Belgian contract rifle, the first firearm to feature charger loading. (© Royal Armouries PR.6275)

The Mauser C78 'Zig-Zag' revolver. (© Royal Armouries PR.3508)

revolver followed the year afterwards. This, the C78, was a novel design employing zig-zag rotation slots on the cylinder, leading to the nickname 'Zig-Zag' revolver. The C78 was passed over for military selection in favour of the more conventional M79 Reichsrevolver, which was still to be found in service during World War I. Paul Mauser was not deterred by this, however, and personally designed in 1886 what would become the Mauser C87. This was one of a few transitional designs including the Reiger (1889) and the Bittner (1893) that abandoned the revolver principle but retained manual operation, in this case by means of a ring-shaped trigger. None of these designs offered much advantage over the traditional revolver, however, and would be surpassed by the first generation of self-loading pistols.

In 1893, the innovative C93 Borchardt pistol was brought to market by Ludwig Loewe & Cie (later Deutsche Waffen und Munitionsfabriken: DWM). Like the later C96, the Hugo Borchardt-designed C93 employed the 'short recoil' system of operation in which barrel and bolt are locked together to contain the high pressures generated on firing, but are then mechanically unlocked after travelling a short distance. This allows the bolt to move rearwards, extract and eject the empty cartridge case, and then return forward under spring pressure to chamber the next cartridge. Rather than the more conventional reciprocating bolt approach of the C96, the C93 Borchardt utilized a hinged 'toggle-lock' inspired by the internal mechanism of the Maxim machine gun. It was clumsy and expensive to manufacture, however, and no more than 3,000 were ever sold. Even so, it established a safe and effective system of operation for a self-loading pistol, and showed much promise. In 1894 further offerings appeared from the German gunsmith and engineer Theodor Bergmann and the Austrian inventor and small-arms designer Ferdinand Ritter von Mannlicher. Mauser's early ambitions in the field of pistol design seemed thwarted, and it must have seemed that another company was destined to bring the self-loading pistol into the 20th century.

DEVELOPMENT
The Feederle pistol

BEATING THE BORCHARDT

Mauser's handgun breakthrough came from a design team including brothers Fidel, Friedrich and Josef Feederle of the *Versuchabteilung* (V-Abt or experimental workshop), where Fidel was superintendent. Anecdotally, Paul Mauser had (sometime in 1893) forbidden Fidel from working on ideas for a pistol, only to put himself in charge and claim the design as his own. Certainly, the final patent is in Mauser's name only, and he did indeed take sole credit for the design. August Weiss (who joined the design team in 1896) diplomatically wrote that the Feederle brothers 'very closely assisted' Paul Mauser (quoted in Belford & Dunlap 1969: 10). Josef's son also stated that the weapon was known as the 'Feederle pistol' by factory workers. Given that the Feederles worked for Mauser, however, none of this is particularly unusual. A letter from author Jon Speed's collection, dated 25 January 1894, from Fidel to Paul (who had a close working relationship) reinforces Fidel's key design role, but also shows that Mauser oversaw development from a very early design stage.

As to any corporate disinterest in developing a Mauser-branded pistol, research by the firearms historians and authors Mauro Baudino and Gerben van Vlimmeren suggests that this came from Loewe, Mauser's parent company, which at the time favoured its own C93 Borchardt design. Mauser was convinced that the company was working against him and appears to have sought the patent at his own cost and without reference to Loewe in order to ensure control of the design. In this he was successful, but in the process he made a number of enemies including Loewe employee Georg Luger, whom he believed was working against him, and another rival, Theodor Bergmann. Bergmann's No. 1 pistol of 1893 was the work of his employee Louis Schmeisser, based upon an 1892 patent by the Hungarian watchmaker Otto Brauswetter. Bergmann claimed to have shared his company's expertise in self-loading pistols with the Mauser company on the understanding that they would put his pistols into production. Instead, they developed their own original design and, he believed, sought a monopoly by means of exclusive patents on the self-loading pistol concept. In fact, the 1895 Mauser patent refers quite specifically to a short-recoil system with a pivoting locking block. Bergmann's pistols would not utilize a similar system (along with C96-style charger loading) until 1897.

Accusations of foul play notwithstanding, Mauser still had to devise a functional weapon. No real design conventions had been established at this early stage in self-loading pistol development. Mauser was first and foremost a rifle manufacturer, and this legacy is evident in the C96 design beyond the wooden shoulder stock, modern machine-made blued-steel parts and slender, tapered barrel (features shared with the C93 Borchardt). Other than the prototype and a few variants, a rifle-style tangent or 'ladder' sight was used, with graduations up to 1,000m. Though this seems ludicrous today, the production C96 was designed to be fitted with its own wooden holster as a shoulder stock, greatly increasing its effective range. Period usage also allowed for such long-range fire (see page 48). Though the Mauser is today perhaps the most famous of the stocked pistols, many of its contemporaries and indeed forebears (as far back as the flintlock era) had been supplied with stocks. The concept has even been attempted since in variants of the Browning GP35 single-action semi-automatic pistol, and into the polymer-frame era in the form of the H&K VP70 double-action machine pistol. The concept has never met with widespread acceptance, however, quite simply because it is rare in an emergency to have time to fit a stock. Even so, at the time it was a desirable feature.

The new pistol required a proven and reliable feed mechanism, and this too was to be rifle-inspired. The C93 experimented (successfully, as it turned out) with a detachable box magazine located conveniently in the grip and retained by a thumb release button. Mauser 'played it safe' by simply scaling down the fixed dual-column magazine pioneered in the company's M1889 (Belgian contract) bolt-action rifle. Although locating this system in front of the grip increased both the length and weight of the weapon, it also increased capacity and still allowed for relatively rapid loading. With the bolt pulled back and held open on the magazine's follower, a charger of ten rounds could be introduced into guides on the barrel extension. All ten cartridges could then be pushed down into the magazine, although this requires practice. Rather than pushing the bolt forward to knock out the empty charger and chamber the first round as in the rifle, the self-loading pistol shooter had only to pull out the charger from the guides to let the bolt fly forward under spring pressure.

The weapon shared a perceived weakness with all self-loading pistols: the need for a well-designed safety mechanism. The pistol market in 1896 was utterly dominated by revolvers. These did not require a manual safety catch, since they either had to be cocked before use (a 'single action' trigger) or required a very long and deliberate trigger pull to cock and

Key members of the Mauser team that designed and produced the Mauser pistol. From top to bottom: Fidel Feederle; August Gaiser; Paul Mauser II; Theodor Schmid; Friedrich Doll. (Gerben van Vlimmeren & Mauro Baudino)

An 1895-dated prototype of the Mauser Self-Loading Pistol, later known as the C96. (Paul Mauser Archive – M. Baudino Collection)

release the hammer (the 'double action' trigger). The hinged 'flap' safety used on Mauser rifles would not translate to the compact pistol, and so a pivoting lever was designed to block the hammer. This was adequate given careful use, but remained a weak point in the design. Mauser was to spend the next several decades attempting to perfect the weapon's awkward safety lever (see page 35).

The trigger was a simple lever that activated the sear. This in turn was built into the heart of the system: the lock frame. The lock frame contained the pistol's main and trigger springs, its hammer, sear bar and a disconnector component to prevent the hammer following the bolt home on each shot (and therefore a malfunction). This sub-assembly sat above the trigger and was connected to the bolt by a pivoting locking block with lugs that engaged with the underside of the bolt when the latter was closed (i.e. forward). These lugs would be pulled out of engagement when the barrel assembly and bolt had travelled a short distance (hence 'short recoil'). The bolt was then free to cycle ready for the next shot. Astonishingly, given the inherent complexity of self-loading designs, no screws, rivets or pins were necessary to hold the pistol together aside from a single screw for the wooden grip panels and a pin (later dispensed with) for the rear sight. All other components were designed to slide, click and lock into each other. The supplied disassembly and cleaning tool was required to strip the bolt, but basic cleaning could be accomplished with a spare cartridge by

The final patent for the new Mauser pistol, German patent 90430, submitted on 11 December 1895. (HECKLER & KOCH GMBH, Publication number EP0505917)

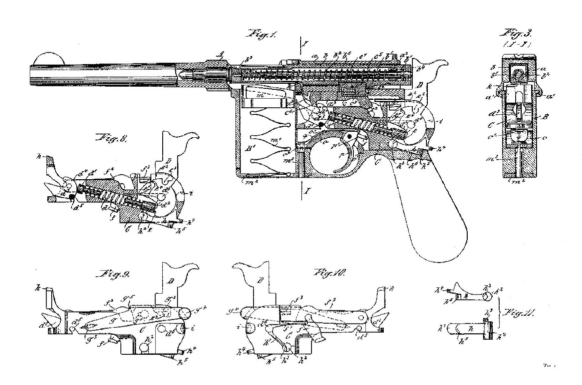

THE 'BROOMHANDLE' EXPOSED

7.63×25mm C96

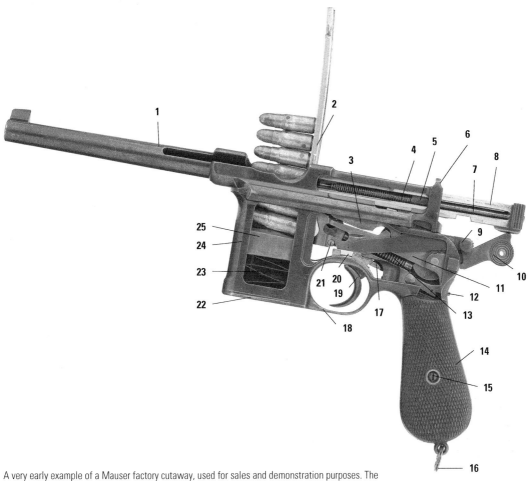

A very early example of a Mauser factory cutaway, used for sales and demonstration purposes. The pre-production C96 is shown here with a ten-round charger inserted and the contents partially loaded into the magazine. (© Royal Armouries PR.11319)

1. Barrel and barrel extension
2. Charger inserted into guides
3. Locking block
4. Recoil spring
5. Recoil spring abutment
6. Rear sight
7. Striker
8. Bolt
9. Safety lever
10. Hammer
11. Lock frame
12. Retaining latch
13. Mainspring and mainspring plunger

14. Grips
15. Grip screw
16. Lanyard ring
17. Disconnector and sear
18. Trigger guard
19. Trigger
20. Trigger spring
21. Coupling and coupling plunger
22. Floor plate
23. Carrier spring (magazine spring)
24. Body (frame)
25. Magazine carrier (follower)

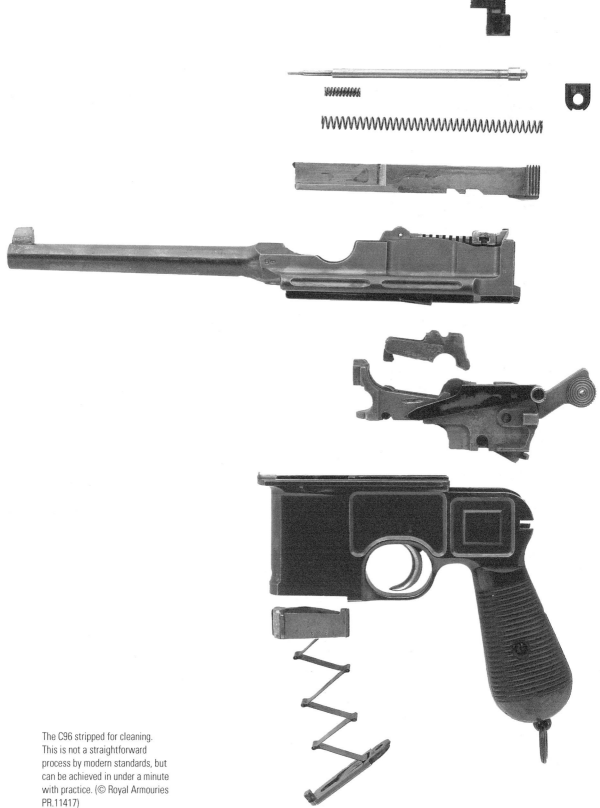

The C96 stripped for cleaning. This is not a straightforward process by modern standards, but can be achieved in under a minute with practice. (© Royal Armouries PR.11417)

depressing the magazine floorplate button and pressing up on the disassembly catch at the rear. The result was a weapon that is at once complex by comparison with modern pistols, but also elegantly simple, containing only 37 parts compared to 59 for the P08 'Luger'. The final design was officially designated the 'Recoil Loader with Locking Block, Self-Loading Pistol C96', and patented in Germany under Paul Mauser's name on 11 December 1895. A series of foreign patents followed, building toward the commercial production and sale of the new pistol.

Weight was a major concern for early self-loading pistols. As refined for mass-production, the standard ten-shot C96 weighed 1,250g. This compared favourably with the C93 Borchardt, but was substantially heavier than the Reichsrevolver and rival designs like the Mannlicher, let alone later more advanced pistols like the P08 'Luger' and Colt M1911. Attempts to reduce the weight of the pre-production pistols were not enough, and so a six-shot variant was designed to fall within 3 per cent of the weight of the then-standard C79 Reichsrevolver (itself a relatively large and hefty handgun). The six-shot variant was substantially (105g) lighter, but sacrificed four rounds' capacity. This meant customers tended to reject it in favour of the ten-shot C96 – if they opted for the Mauser at all. Also offered in this initial product range was a 20-shot variant, but its sheer size and weight also discouraged buyers.

The quality of the early C96 was typical of its time, a pleasing combination of precision machining and careful fitting and finishing by the hands of craftsmen, applying generations of skill and knowledge to each pistol. Steel components were treated with the traditional 'rust bluing' process in which parts were repeatedly coated with an acid, left to rust, then scrubbed and polished until a deep and lustrous blue was achieved. This produced a very corrosion-resistant but also very attractive surface. The extractor, rear sight, safety and firing-pin retaining pieces were 'fire blued', giving a bright, slight oil-slick appearance. The trigger

Mauser 7.63×25mm ammunition in a charger. The cartridge selected for the C96 was the existing 7.65×25mm designed by Borchardt for his C93 pistol. It is not widely appreciated that the Mauser's acclaimed 7.63×25mm cartridge was actually Borchardt's, a clear result of the relative popularity of the two types. Indeed, despite their names, the 7.65×25mm Borchardt, 7.63×25mm Mauser and the later 7.62×25mm Tokarev are all dimensionally the same cartridge, each iteration being loaded to a higher pressure than the last. Aside from a minor name change, the difference between the now-obsolete Borchardt cartridge and the Mauser 7.63×25mm that remains in production today is simply that the stronger Mauser action allowed ammunition manufacturers to load 'hotter' rounds. This pushed muzzle velocities from around 385m/sec to 425m/sec, increasing the effectiveness of the round and contributing to later celebrations of the C96's superior penetration. (© Royal Armouries XX.716)

The huge 20-shot C96 next to its bulky enlarged stock-holster. This was not a practical handgun. (Courtesy Leonardo M. Antaris, MD)

was 'strawed' or heated until slightly coloured. Internal parts and the hammer were case-hardened (though not multi-coloured like a Colt revolver frame), increasing their carbon content and resulting in a dull

THE 'CONEHAMMER' REVEALED

7.63×25mm C96

A C96 'Conehammer' fully stripped to its component parts, 1897. The only screw is for the grips. (© Royal Armouries PR.11417)

1. Barrel and barrel extension
2. Locking block
3. Recoil spring
4. Recoil spring abutment
5. Striker
6. Retractor spring
7. Extractor
8. Bolt
9. Firing pin retaining plate (early models)
10. Lock frame
11. Hammer
12. Hammer pin
13. Safety lever
14. Disconnector
15. Sear
16. Mainspring
17. Mainspring plunger
18. Coupling plunger
19. Coupling
20. Retaining latch
21. Body (frame)
22. Magazine carrier (floorplate)
23. Carrier spring
24. Floor plate
25. Floor plate locking pin
26. Trigger and (early models) trigger insert and pin
27. Trigger spring
28. Grips
29. Grip screw
30. Sight leaf
31. Sight leaf spring
32. Slide
33. Slide catch
34. Catch spring
35. Rear-sight pin (early models)
36. Lanyard ring

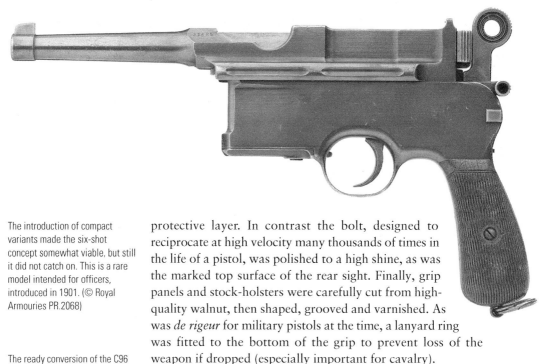

protective layer. In contrast the bolt, designed to reciprocate at high velocity many thousands of times in the life of a pistol, was polished to a high shine, as was the marked top surface of the rear sight. Finally, grip panels and stock-holsters were carefully cut from high-quality walnut, then shaped, grooved and varnished. As was *de rigeur* for military pistols at the time, a lanyard ring was fitted to the bottom of the grip to prevent loss of the weapon if dropped (especially important for cavalry).

A number of early C96s were presented to senior German military officials between June and August 1896. The War Minister was sufficiently impressed to suggest that the new stocked pistol should replace carbine rifles then in military service. Kaiser Wilhelm II himself was presented with a specially inscribed pistol following a personal demonstration of both pistol and carbine, and seems to have been suitably impressed. Despite this early positivity, however, no government contracts were signed. It is perhaps telling that the Kaiser's response to the demonstration was to request a self-loading military rifle on the same principle (an application to which the C96 action proved unsuited). Orders for the pistol from both civilian and military spheres picked up as the 20th century approached, however, and for a short time at least, the Mauser dominated the small self-loading pistol market. The C93 Borchardt had great promise but needed a radical redesign, while contemporary offerings from Mannlicher and Bergmann were severely underpowered. Yet Mauser continued to make changes.

A BIGGER HAMMER

The most obvious change made to the C96 over the years was the style of hammer fitted, and changes to this form the basis of collector categorization. Yet, useful as these changes are to us today, it is not definitively known why Mauser chose to move from the chunkier 'cone' hammer (named for its two lateral grooved grasping cones), to the hollow 'large ring' (from 1899) and later 'small ring' (1904 onwards) hammers, both of which featured serrations on their upper surface to aid in cocking. Presumably feedback suggested that a smaller hammer was easy enough to operate, leading Mauser to fractionally reduce the weight, bulk, and manufacturing cost of the weapon. Savings (especially between 'large' and 'small' rings) cannot have been significant, however.

Cost was certainly an issue in the extensive machining work required to create the major assemblies. With this in mind, various features were simplified. The 'step' in the barrel was eliminated within the first couple of years of production. In 1899, as part of the Italian contract, and coinciding with the move to the 'large ring' hammer, the early separate trigger assembly was disposed of and the trigger was instead hung directly from the frame. A new firing pin was designed that did not require the use of a special tool for stripping, and the sight no longer required a separate pin. Most noticeably, at this time Mauser ceased milling out the distinctive deep recessed panels. These were reinstated in 1902, initially to only half

The so-called 'Bolo' variant of the C96. The shorter barrel and grip frame create a handier, if rather squat-looking weapon. (© Royal Armouries PR.7522)

the previous depth, but in 1904 full depth was achieved once again. Mauser seems to have been experimenting, but to no clear end. Weight was certainly not the concern, since both 'flatside' and half-depth panel milled frames were machined on the inside to compensate. In any case, with the addition of a strengthened (shorter and wider) extractor in 1905, the first definitive pattern (sometimes called the 'Pre-war Commercial') was created. This was further improved by the incorporation of the 'New Safety' (see page 36) in 1912 (the so-called 'Wartime Commercial' and its 9mm variant for the German military, the 'Prussian Contract'). These variations covered the bulk of production, with hundreds of thousands manufactured between 1905 and 1930.

Defeat in World War I hit German arms manufacturers hard. The Treaty of Versailles placed limits on the number and nature of firearms that could be manufactured, sold and exported, including pistols. This did not halt firearms development entirely, however, as rebuilding the shattered post-war German economy relied upon maintaining and expanding exports, including the arms for which Germany was known. Mauser found itself rebuilding existing pistols to the new standard which, in an attempt to limit the number of militarily viable arms (i.e. rifles and machine guns), stipulated a barrel no longer than 100mm. Existing pistols were reworked with shortened barrels and stamped with the property mark '1920' (these are known today by collectors as 'Weimar reworks'). Some were even fitted with 'Luger' barrels, giving them a distinctive hybrid appearance. There was no ban on the export of non-military arms,

The M1930 pistol. In an odd throwback to the original C96 prototype, the barrel featured a machined step. The new finish was a very dark (almost black), lustrous blue. A few apparently cost-saving measures were taken, however. The barrel was slightly shorter (132mm instead of 140mm), and a simplified hammer omitted the former inner 'ring'. Lightening cuts to the interior of the grip frame were omitted, as was internal polishing of the lock frame (originally done to smooth the trigger pull). As production progressed, the earlier deep lateral grooves were also omitted from the exterior of the barrel extension. The grip frame was slightly enlarged, with subtly different grips fitted (12 grooves instead of 23). None of this did anything to improve the M1930's ergonomics. In fact the final M1930 is about 70g heavier than a pre-war commercial pistol, and even more of a handful due to chunkier grip panels that dig into the web of a smaller hand and cramp the knuckle of a larger one. (© Royal Armouries PR.2072)

Mauser's first patent for a fully automatic pistol, dated 17 June 1921. (Weapons Mauser Ag. Publication number US1427097 A)

however, and lucrative markets were still to be exploited. For commercial sale, therefore, Mauser also revived a style originally offered for sale in 1902 with a 99mm barrel and a fixed-notch rear sight for close-quarters use. This also had a shorter grip frame, making for a substantially lighter and handier pistol. The type would later be dubbed 'Bolo' after the Russian Bolshevik revolutionaries said to favour this predominant inter-war variant.

As the enforcement of inter-war restrictions eased, a final redesign of the standard pistol took place, resulting in the M1930. Although a redesign in almost every detail, it is virtually identical to the earlier patterns. Rather than seeking to bring the C96 into the 20th century in terms of ease and cost of production, the new pistol was if anything a return to the high standard of craftsmanship seen in pre-war guns. The only meaningful change was in the safety (see page 36). It is tempting to see the M1930 as a rebranding exercise intended to shed the 19th-century image of the design, similar to Winchester's renaming of its series of rifles to omit the telltale design year ('Model 92' instead of 'Model 1892' for example). Beyond this, the M1930 and its fully automatic M712 Schnellfeuer stablemate reflect the growing confidence of Germany as a resurgent nation. It also shows Mauser's reliance on the old C96, however, in lieu of a worthy successor and rival to the P08 'Luger' and Walther P38.

RAPID FIRE

Given the built-in controllability and high capacity of the (stocked) C96, and the World War I debut of the submachine gun, the obvious next step was to convert the design to fire fully automatically. Contrary to received wisdom, the first fully automatic variant of the C96 was actually designed at Mauser – original C96 co-designer Fidel Feederle pioneered the concept with US patent 1,427,097, filed as early as 1921 – and not, as is usually claimed, by rival company Unceta y Cía in Spain. Indeed, the Spanish pistols followed a completely different internal design. The only feature to be carried over is the detachable box magazine, though this too is of a different pattern. Although provision is made for full-automatic fire, no selector switch is shown or described, and the patent description optimistically suggests that the user may select single shots or continuous fire by trigger control alone. In practice this would have been impossible.

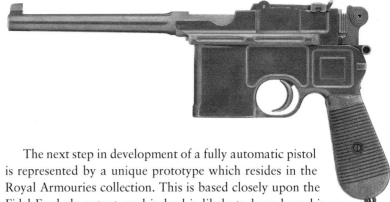

The little-known 1920s prototype of what became the M712 Schnellfeuer machine pistol. (© Royal Armouries PR.10739)

The next step in development of a fully automatic pistol is represented by a unique prototype which resides in the Royal Armouries collection. This is based closely upon the Fidel Feederle patent, and indeed is likely to have been his own work or built under his supervision. It has a lock frame designed to permit semi- and full-automatic fire, but a fire-selector lever has been added to the right-hand side with the markings 'E' (*Einzelfeuer* or 'single fire') and 'R' (*Reihenfeuer* or 'serial fire'). The weapon functions satisfactorily when operation is simulated in semi- and full-automatic modes; and the selector cannot easily be operated inadvertently, although the pistol's reliability with live ammunition could not be assessed (this being a unique museum-piece). The pistol is marked on the left panel 'Konstr. 4.10.26', two years before the Astra M901 (see page 62), commonly supposed to be the first of its type. Like other prototypes and cutaway examples, it bears a serial number in its own range, in this case serial no. 1.

In the event Mauser opted not to proceed with the project, most likely due to lack of funds in the difficult post-war German economy. It was left to Astra to fill this small but potentially lucrative niche in the market. The success of the automatic variants of the Astra M900 (from 1928) forced Mauser to look again, but Fidel Feederle's design was not resurrected. Instead, Austrian Josef Nickl, an in-house Mauser designer, came up with a totally new system quite different from its Mauser and Unceta y Cía predecessors. Nickl's pistol was patented, rapidly put into production and 1,000 examples shipped to China, all in 1931. Unlike those earlier designs,

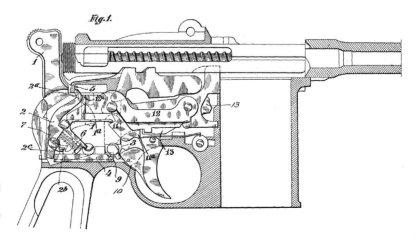

The final Karl Westinger-designed form of the M712 Schnellfeuer. (Weapons Mauser Ag. Publication number US1427097 A)

Nickl's pistol featured a large and prominent lever on the left side, operated by the thumb of the firing hand. This arrangement was convenient, but would have been prone to accidental full-automatic discharge if the lever were caught when drawing the pistol, or inadvertently left on the wrong setting by the shooter.

A lack of factory records from the period means that we cannot be sure why the Nickl design was deemed to be unsatisfactory. Whatever the reason, the gun was replaced only a year (and 5,000 pistols) later by an internally simpler and externally safer mechanism conceived by Karl Westinger. Westinger was another noted designer who would go on to co-found (with Ernst Altenburger) the sporting firearms company Feinwerkbau. His new definitive pattern was closely based upon Nickl's work, but incorporated two simple yet important changes. First, the complex laterally acting automatic sear was replaced by a simplified, vertically acting 'catch hook'. Secondly, a new wedge-shaped selector switch required that a button be depressed before the selector switch could be rotated. The new M712 Schnellfeuer was a success, with roughly 100,000 guns produced and sold around the world, as opposed to just 13,000 of the rival Astra variants. Most select-fire 'Broomhandle'-style pistols went to the Chinese market that so enjoyed them.

THE END OF THE LINE

In one sense the C96 was a victim of its own success. Mauser's renewed attempts to secure German military contracts with its M1906/08 failed, and even the company's successful range of pocket pistols never matched the sales of the C96. Mauser could not rely upon the increasingly obsolescent 'Broomhandle', but neither could the company design a replacement. In 1930 Mauser began production of another iconic pistol and, as with the 'Broomhandle', would go on to produce one million examples. This time, however, it was not a Mauser design but their old rival, the P08 'Luger'. As a result of this, new production of the 'Broomhandle' is thought to have ceased by 1936, although guns were assembled from parts for another several years until the outbreak of World War II finally brought down the curtain on this famous weapon. Ultimately, Mauser produced around one million C96s over the 43 years from 1896 to 1939.

A German-made M712 Schnellfeuer with Chinese export markings. (© Royal Armouries PR.7524)

USE
A global success story

SEEKING MILITARY ADOPTION

Breaking into the market

Despite innovative design, reliable function and firepower superior to that of contemporary pistols, not to mention the industrial and marketing clout of the Mauser company, the C96 struggled to win significant military contracts. In September 1905, Spanish authorities rejected the Mauser in favour of the Bergmann-Bayard M1903; and a potentially lucrative deal with Mexico (c.1909) was cancelled at an advanced stage, with a few pistols already made and marked accordingly. Mauser's most obvious customer was the German Empire, which almost immediately ordered a small quantity (145) sufficient to conduct evaluation and limited troop trials. The first of these did not arrive until 1898, and trials were

A 'flatside' pistol procured for German Army trials in 1902. Some of the trial pistols were issued to officers, NCOs and government officials on the German East Asiatic expedition. The experience of the pistol on this German military aid effort to China (at the time of the Boxer Rebellion) does not seem to have been a good one, but may have helped to spark Chinese fascination with the 'Box Cannon', as they later called it. This is reflected in a later (1915) account by a German pilot who offered his service pistol as a gift to a delighted local official. (Courtesy of King Rhoton)

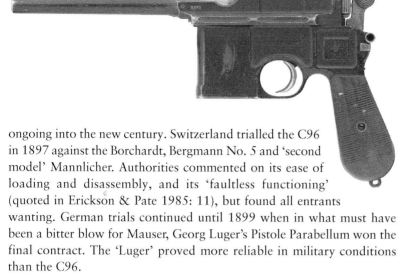

ongoing into the new century. Switzerland trialled the C96 in 1897 against the Borchardt, Bergmann No. 5 and 'second model' Mannlicher. Authorities commented on its ease of loading and disassembly, and its 'faultless functioning' (quoted in Erickson & Pate 1985: 11), but found all entrants wanting. German trials continued until 1899 when in what must have been a bitter blow for Mauser, Georg Luger's Pistole Parabellum won the final contract. The 'Luger' proved more reliable in military conditions than the C96.

Nevertheless, the Ottoman Empire expressed early interest. Whether privately or officially procured, Turkish Mausers also saw active service. Observers in Armenia in 1914 noted the Mausers carried by the Turks directing arrests and interrogations, and T.E. Lawrence wrote of receiving a flesh wound in the hip from a string of 7.63mm bullets fired by a senior officer from the window of an Ottoman train that Lawrence had ambushed.

The various design changes made in 1899, including the 'flatside' frame, had been prompted by a promising order from the Italian Navy, which had procured pistols for trial as early as 1897. The C96 was adopted under the service name 'Pistole L'arme Automatiche modello sous 1899', and 5,000 were purchased. After this promising start, interest faltered. The Italian contract was not completed until 1905, and the only follow-on order made by that country was for an additional 250 pistols. In fact, Italy, with its long and proud history of firearms design, was by this time on the way to producing its own military service pistol, the Glisenti M1910.

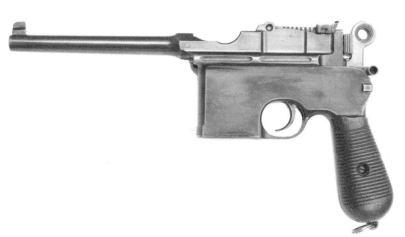

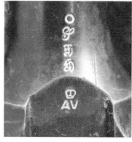

Into the East

By 1900 Mauser was seeking to increase the appeal of the C96 by offering an even more potent chambering. In 1904 the company released pistols chambered for a 'necked up' variant of the 7.63mm cartridge popularly dubbed '9mm Mauser Export'. This long and powerful cartridge was a handful to shoot and was largely unsuccessful. It was easily outperformed by DWM's 9mm Parabellum. Government sales of the C96 in either calibre remained in the doldrums, and production of the 9mm Export pistols would cease in 1914. The next military contract did not arrive until 1908, when the Siamese (Thai) government purchased a small (unknown) quantity of 7.63mm weapons. Another small order of about 1,000 pistols came from Persia in 1911. These bear a Persian royal crest and proof mark on the left side of the barrel extension.

The C96 was popular among Persians generally, from civilians to security forces, to the many paramilitaries operating there during World War I. Major-General Lionel C. Dunsterville, commander of the small British detachment known as 'Dunsterforce', described the local fighting men as 'fierce-looking and heavily-armed warriors. With successive bandoliers of cartridges arranged round their bodies so as to form a very showy waistcoat, Mauser pistol on waistbelt and rifle in hand' (Dunsterville 1920: 50). These men were joined later by Caucasian revolutionaries, well-armed with modern Mauser rifles and pistols which they used to attack government installations and the Russian detachments established to protect them. Another account, from journalist David Fraser, makes clear that the firepower of the Mauser was used in a rather haphazard manner akin to the tactics of present-day insurgent and paramilitary forces:

> On the way back I got mixed up with a fight in the Ala-ed-Dowleh, the street of the Legations. A party of Caucasians and Armenians darted

past, taking cover in doorways and behind trees as they advanced. They got within close range of the Cossack lines, against which they directed a heavy rifle fire, followed by a deluge of Mauser pistol bullets. A fierce return fire forced them to retire, for which I was thankful, as watching this sort of work was attended by more danger than the excitement was worth. (Fraser 1910: 124)

Evidence like this from various countries suggests that the big pistol was seen as a prestige weapon or even a badge of rank, often worn prominently on the front of the body. It was at once large and noisy enough to impress, but small enough to carry all day in its built-in holster.

The C96 was also popular elsewhere in the Middle East region. In Pakistan as recently as the 1950s, a tribal fighter was filmed proudly

THIS PAGE & OPPOSITE
Three views of a decorated six-shot pistol chambered for the 9mm Mauser Export cartridge. The stock is extensively carved. (G. Sturgess Collection)

The Persian C96 and its distinctive royal crest marking. (Courtesy of King Rhoton)

displaying his stocked Mauser for American filmmaker Glenn Foster and his Afghan cameraman Hajji Mehtabuddin. The type also saw limited use in Israel when the nascent state was obliged to make use of a wide range of military equipment in the course of its establishment and for some time afterwards. Markings on a surviving example show that the C96 was among the firearms carried, although little is known about the extent of Israeli use of the type, or the source of these examples. They may, like other weapons used by the state, have been captured German examples. C96s had been somewhat common in the Middle East, however. In 1913, Jewish Galician settler Salomon Dyk used Mauser and Browning pistols to defend his settlement from Arab attack. In any case, the sheer variety of pistol sizes, shapes, calibres and safety devices in use led the Israeli forces to carry pistols loaded, hammer down, with an empty chamber. This rendered them safe when not needed, and made training on different types quicker and easier. The stiff bolt of the C96 would certainly not have lent itself to this sort of practice, however, and the weapon would have been extremely difficult to get into action quickly.

Whether carried as a sidearm or as a primary weapon, and whatever its practical advantages, the Mauser was favoured by anyone wishing to cut an intimidating figure. One 1920s account from war-torn Hungary (in present-day Slovakia) describes an officer of the Russian 'Red Guards' armed with two C96s, one in each hand, as he boarded a boat to inspect its foreign passengers. We can only speculate as to whether these were examples of the compact 'Bolo' supposedly favoured by Bolshevik users such as this man. In reality, the Bolsheviks had no monopoly on the C96, and both sides made extensive use of it during the Russian Civil War (1917–22) that precipitated these events.

This C96 pistol, serial number 161474, was the weapon of Bolshevik terrorist and 'Deputy Regional Commissar of Justice' Pyotr Yermakov. Although the C96 was just as eagerly used by counter-revolutionary forces, it is the 'Bolos' who are best remembered today. This is in part due to the actions of Yermakov, whose love of the C96 was such that he was nicknamed 'Comrade Mauser'. On 17 July 1918 he used his full-sized 7.63mm C96 to shoot Empress Alexandra Feodorovna in the head during the mass execution of the exiled Romanov family at Ekaterinburg. Yermakov emptied his Mauser and drew a back-up pistol to continue his part in the massacre. He is also thought to have killed Grand Duchesses Olga, Maria and Anastasia. (Courtesy of Paul Gilbert @ Royal Russia)

Ushomyr, Ukraine, April 1920: Polish troops involved in the Kiev Offensive of the Soviet–Polish War (1919–21). The soldier in the centre has his C96 – perhaps captured from the Poles' Russian enemies – unholstered and stocked ready for action. The Bolshevik takeover of Russia led to the ceding of Ukraine to the Central Powers, and the rise of an Anarcho-Communist nationalist movement there. Here, too, the C96 was a popular weapon and status symbol, notably carried by Revolutionary Insurrectionary Army of Ukraine commander Fedir Shchus, shot dead by Russian Cossacks in 1921. (© IWM Q 92200)

The 'Broomhandle' in Africa

Our best period sources for military use of the C96 relate not to the official contract guns, but instead come from British Army officers on campaign in the Sudan (*c*.1898) and in South Africa (1899–1902). These men were obliged to purchase their own sidearms, and many of them selected the Mauser over the standard .455-calibre Webley revolver. In a timely move, famous London gunmaker Westley Richards had in 1897 obtained exclusive dealer rights to the C96 in Britain. The firm began sales to the trade and to the public in 1898, just in time to market the pistol to British officers about to depart for Africa. The weapon was successful enough that these rights were jealously guarded, and Westley Richards intervened when other dealers attempted to breach this arrangement. Records show that 7,901 examples were sold by Westley Richards between 1897 and 1905, with brisk sales soaring into the thousands but then dropping back again after the Second Anglo-Boer War to around 100 per year by 1905. The demand was clearly the result of interest from military men, in parallel with steady sales to civilians. By comparison, the Webley & Scott company, dominant in both military and civilian sales, sold 14,008 Mk IV revolvers in the year 1900 alone. It is fair to say that at this point in its history, the C96 was a niche product, a status symbol for those 'in the know' about modern firearms.

Easily the most famous proponent of the C96 was future British Prime Minister Winston Spencer Churchill, who purchased his first example in London on 25 July 1898, just prior to departing for the Sudan. In his 1899 book *The River War*, Churchill sang the C96's praises as a sidearm superior in every way to both the revolver and other self-loading pistols. In a letter to his mother he described it as 'the best thing in the world'

Westley Richards offered the C96 not only with its Mauser-supplied holster-stock case, but also with this traditional wooden pistol case complete with compartments for tools and pre-loaded chargers. (Courtesy Leonardo M. Antaris, MD)

(quoted in Manchester 1984: 279). Indeed, Churchill was so impressed with the 'Broomhandle' that he apparently purchased another four examples on his return to Britain later in 1898. Research by Mauro Baudino and Gerben van Vlimmeren has established these pistols as serial numbers 3511, 2373, 4257 and 13769. At least one accompanied Churchill to South Africa and narrowly avoided capture when he was briefly made a prisoner of the Boers. Unfortunately, it appears that none of these important artefacts have survived to the present, but Churchill did provide rare insight into the C96 as a fighting pistol in his autobiography *My Early Life*. Having chosen the Mauser in part because of a polo-inflicted dislocated shoulder that prevented effective use of the cavalry sword, he later recognized that had he relied upon the sword at the battle of Omdurman (2 September 1898), he may not have lived to tell the tale. Churchill's account of this battle, in which he fought as a lieutenant in the 21st Lancers, is striking:

> I had the impression of scattered Dervishes running to and fro in all directions. Straight before me a man threw himself on the ground. The reader must remember that I had been trained as a cavalry soldier to believe that if ever cavalry broke into a mass of infantry, the latter would be at their mercy. My first idea therefore was that the man was terrified. But simultaneously I saw the gleam of his curved sword as he drew it back for a ham-stringing cut. I had room and time enough to turn my pony out of his reach, and leaning over on the off side I fired two shots into him at about three yards. As I straightened myself in the saddle, I saw before me another figure with uplifted sword. I raised my pistol and fired. So close were we that the pistol itself actually struck him. Man and sword disappeared below and behind me. On my left, ten yards away, was an Arab horseman in a bright-coloured tunic and steel helmet, with chain-mail hangings. I fired at him. He turned aside. (Churchill 1930: 190)

Winston.

Lieutenant-Colonel Edward Bethune, commander of Bethune's Horse in the Second Anglo-Boer War, 1902. Having lost his right arm in India, Bethune wears his stock-holster on his left side, butt rearmost. (Print Collector/Print Collector/Getty Images)

Disordered by the charge, Churchill's unit began to regroup. At this point he was obliged to use his pistol again:

> Suddenly in the midst of the troop up sprang a Dervish. How he got there I do not know. He must have leaped out of some scrub or hole. All the troopers turned upon him thrusting with their lances: but he darted to and fro causing for the moment a frantic commotion. Wounded several times, he staggered towards me raising his spear. I shot him at less than a yard. He fell on the sand, and lay there dead. How easy to kill a man! But I did not worry about it. I found I had fired the whole magazine of my Mauser pistol, so I put in a new clip of ten cartridges before thinking of anything else. (Churchill 1930: 190)

Churchill had killed at least five men with his ten rounds. In this action he had wielded his C96 one-handed as a pistol, but as a war correspondent two years later at Kopjes Station in South Africa, he highlighted the advantage inherent in a detachable shoulder stock:

While I was standing on the foot-plate to make sure the soldiers had got back into the train, I saw, less than a hundred yards away in the dry water course under the burning bridge, a cluster of dark figures. These were the last Boers I was to see as enemies. I fitted the wooden stock to the Mauser pistol and fired six or seven times at them. They scattered without firing back. (Churchill 1930: 191)

Churchill was not unusual in favouring this new pistol. In 1901 Kitchener, at that time General Officer Commanding-in-Chief (South Africa), responded to a request by the government's Small Arms Committee with: 'though some officers condemn it, the general opinion seems to be that it is a more suitable weapon than a revolver, to be carried by an Officer' (WO Paper 7101/B/6401). A Lieutenant-Colonel Watts of 2nd Battalion, The Prince of Wales's Own (West Yorkshire Regiment), gave specific feedback, saying that 'its accuracy, rapidity of loading and firing, makes it the best description of pistol or revolver for an Infantry or Mounted Infantry Officer' (WO Paper 7101/B/6401). Another officer, Second Lieutenant John Seymour Mellor of the Sussex Militia, was apparently so taken with the C96 that he purchased one following his return from South Africa, perhaps as a replacement for another lost on campaign. Mellor was awarded the Queen's South Africa Medal, and after serving with The King's Royal Rifle Corps, went on to hold senior military and government posts.

A US Army observer, Captain S.L'H. Slocum of the 8th Cavalry, agreed with his British counterparts. Slocum stated: 'The Mauser automatic pistol, which can be used either from the hand or the shoulder, carried by some of the officers, is a most excellent weapon'; perhaps tellingly, he went on to qualify that 'with a larger bullet [it] is better than any form of revolver that I have seen' (Anon 1901: 225). Slocum refers to

BELOW
'Large ring' C96 pistol serial 32752 (1903), belonging to John Seymour Mellor. (© Royal Armouries PR.10770)

BELOW LEFT
John Seymour Mellor as adjutant of the Eton Officer Training Corps, 1913. (Andrew Pay)

29

the heavier, expanding bullets then available (see page 52). By no means all American officers were convinced, however, but many did carry privately purchased C96s on campaign in the Spanish–American War (1898) and in the Philippine–American War (1899–1902). These men clearly preferred the modern Mauser to the much-maligned service-issue Colt M1894, whose .38 Long Colt cartridge propelled a larger and heavier bullet than the Mauser, but at around 770ft/sec (235m/sec) – nearly half the velocity of the Mauser. Regardless of the truth behind reports of the .38 failing to stop Moro tribesman and the greater penetration offered by the Mauser, the latter did carry an additional four rounds over the revolver – perhaps sufficient to carry a gunfight.

Colonial officers, too, opted to carry C96s in South Africa. In July 1900, during sporadic fighting near Berkshire Hill, a Lieutenant Staughton discovered another advantage to the Mauser's unusual holster-stock and solid steel construction. While Staughton was leading a detachment of the Victorian Mounted Rifles, a number of Boers opened fire from concealment. Several rifle bullets blasted through his haversack and one through his helmet, all fortunately missing his torso and head. Another shot struck him in the left side, but his pistol and its holster acted together to serve as inadvertent body armour, stopping the bullet. The weapon was destroyed, but Staughton's life was saved. In Canada, famous 'Mountie' turned soldier Sir Samuel Benfield 'Sam' Steele recommended adoption of the C96 as a mounted-police weapon on his return from service in the Second Anglo-Boer War. Steele had formed a positive view of the weapon as commanding officer of Strathcona's Horse during that conflict. He went on to lead the South African Constabulary and became a senior military officer during World War I. Steele had been the third man to enrol in the North West Mounted Police (reaching the rank of superintendent).

Though there was no formal adoption of the Mauser pistol by British or Imperial forces, small quantities were in fact purchased by the British War Office for issue. It is not known exactly how many were procured, but examples may be encountered today with 'broad arrow' government ownership and 'sold out of service' marks. Despite this limited official issue, extensive unofficial usage and numerous favourable reports – many of which had actually been directly solicited by personnel of the War Office, who were clearly intrigued by the C96 – the British authorities never comparatively trialled it as a Webley revolver replacement. As such, no large-scale contract was forthcoming from the UK. This was doubtless due to the stated concerns over rank-and-file competence, as well as the

OPPOSITE
Boer fighters often carved decoration and battle honours into their rifle stocks. This C96 has had its stock similarly decorated by a British officer of The Royal Scots Fusiliers, including an inset coin of the South African Republic (ZAR). (© Royal Armouries XII.10246)

British officers posing for the camera somewhere in South Africa, c.1900. Most carry Webley revolvers, but the man on the right aims a C96 into the distance. (© TopFoto 1292956)

higher cost, foreign origin, and small calibre of the weapon. Wartime exigencies permitted the use of non-standard cartridges, but once the South African war had concluded, officers would have been obliged to keep their private purchases to the .455 service calibre only, ruling out the C96 even for use by officers.

Amid all this enthusiasm, there was concern that inexperienced users might struggle to safely operate the C96. For some officers, this meant cavalry troopers, artillerymen, drivers or any soldiers of the 'other ranks' requiring an issue pistol. This prejudice was demonstrated by Lieutenant-Colonel A.H. Edwards of the Imperial Light Horse, who reported in May 1902 to the Director General of Ordnance that he had chosen not to issue C96s to his unit during the Second Anglo-Boer War. Among a long list of personal gripes, he claimed that 'The weapon, even in the hands of those who profess to understand its mechanism, is a dangerous one, and quite unsuited on that account, if for no other, for issue to the rank and file of a regiment' (WO Paper 7101/B/6582A). Troopers in another (Yeomanry) regiment were prohibited from carrying Mausers and other pistols that they had purchased for use on campaign. This class divide was not always so rigidly enforced, however. One dispatch-rider was ordered to convey a message quietly by means of a khaki-painted Raleigh bicycle. Rather than a bulky rifle, he was provided with a Mauser pistol, with which he was obliged to return fire when he came under rifle fire near a drift in the Renoster Spruit.

Britain's Boer enemies also favoured the Mauser. *Harper's Magazine* for July 1900 reported on an incident in which four Boers were surrounded near Ladysmith by a force of 700 British soldiers. Offered the option of surrender, they instead drew their Mauser pistols. With these they were able to fend off the attackers sufficiently to be able to bring their rifles into play as well. They were apparently able to kill, wound and suppress, allowing their comrades time to respond to the attack. Aside from the apparent firepower advantage that their C96s gave them, it is noteworthy that all four men were armed with the type.

Safety concerns

It was during British combat usage of the C96 that the deficiencies of the safety catch became apparent. Mauser's design intent had been for the user to load the pistol, make ready, and apply the safety catch. In the British report, several officers praised this ability to carry 'at full cock' ready for immediate action. The first-generation safety catch was extremely stiff, however, and had to be pushed upwards to disengage it – hardly a natural effort for the firing hand. There was also so little travel in the lever that it was difficult to discern quickly whether it was in the up (fire) or down (safe) position. Swiss trials deemed it too indistinct, and it does seem to have caused problems in the field. In a skirmish that took place on 24 January 1900 between 2nd Battalion, The Lancashire Fusiliers and Boer forces, Colonel A. Court 'tried to use his Mauser pistol, but in this critical moment found the safety catch was set, and had to snatch up a great stone, with which he felled his opponent' (Wilson 1900: 286). This incident is eerily similar to one recounted by Robert Graves in his biography of T.E. Lawrence. During his archaeological expedition to Syria in 1909, Lawrence asked a stranger for directions and was attacked by him, his pistol taken. Lawrence's life was saved only by the inability of his Turkmen assailant to take off the safety catch, which being the second type was in the raised (on) position. In this story Lawrence was the one felled by a stone and subsequently mugged. The pistol and his other possessions were recovered by local police.

In theory, the safety could be ignored and other procedures used. Indeed, if drawn from the wooden holster, the pistol had to be left uncocked in order to close the lid. The solution was to make ready the pistol and then carefully lower the hammer for safe carriage. This was Winston Churchill's preferred mode of carry, but as he relates in his autobiography, even cocking the hammer alone might be difficult in an emergency, especially for cavalry at the gallop. The weapon might even discharge accidentally if the hammer slipped from the fingers during this delicate operation. The potential for negligent discharges led one man to condemn the many C96s in service as 'the infernal Mauser pistols' (Cadogan 1908: 54).

A redesign was needed, and after failed experimentation with the complicated *Gelenksicherung* ('link safety') of 1902, which cocked the hammer when raised but left it cocked when lowered, a second-pattern safety catch was introduced in 1905. This had a longer travel and was pushed down instead of up to make the pistol ready to fire. It was a step in the right direction, albeit confusing for 'early adopters' used to the opposite arrangement. It was easy to apply accidentally, however, and there were also complaints from German military servicemen. With this safety, if the trigger was pulled with the safety almost 'off', the hammer could slip off the sear, being held back only by the safety. When the shooter realized that the weapon had not fired and tried again to take the safety off, he would inadvertently discharge the weapon, quite possibly in an unsafe direction. This continuing unsafe reputation prompted British staff officer Frederic Coleman to write in 1916:

C96 safety catches

In all of these images, the safety is OFF. The 'first pattern' (**1**) is pushed *down* for 'on' (© Royal Armouries PR.11417). The second pattern (**2**) is pushed *up* for 'on' (© Royal Armouries PR.10770). The 'New Safety' (**3**) is pushed up for 'on', but ONLY if the hammer is pulled partly or all the way back (© Royal Armouries XII.5785). The 'Universal' version (**4**), pushed up for 'on', can be applied with hammer down or cocked, and allows decocking by means of trigger pull (© Royal Armouries PR.2072).

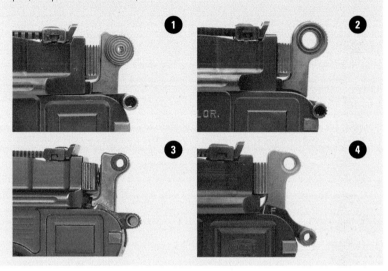

We were told the forest was full of Uhlan scouts, who had been seen crossing the road, but we were apparently in quite as much danger from Jimmy Rothschild's Mauser pistol, which he loaded and carried at the 'ready', until both Kirkwood and I demanded that he should keep it pointed in the direction of the enemy rather than towards the back of our heads. (Coleman 1916: 61)

Inevitably, a third design dubbed the *Neuer Sicherung* (New Safety) was introduced *c*.1915, the hammer being clearly marked with the interleaved letters 'NS' to limit confusion. This solved existing problems but introduced another: the safety could not be applied without pulling the hammer slightly back – a two-handed operation. This problem was in turn fixed in the fourth and final 'Universal' safety built into the M1930 and subsequently the M712 Schnellfeuer. This directly blocked the sear rather than simply holding back the hammer (which also prevented firing when dropped), had clear 'F' and 'S' markings, and could be easily engaged with the firing hand. With the benefit of hindsight, it is easily the most practical design, even if the new decocking feature required that the trigger be pulled when the safety was applied (potentially dangerous). It seems likely that the safety lever was an important factor in limiting military and indeed law-enforcement adoption of the C96. Most were familiar with the foolproof double-action revolver with its very safe long and heavy trigger pull. Yet for the time being, the military market remained Mauser's big hope.

OPPOSITE
Leutnant Georg Sellnick of Kgl. Sächs. Reserve-Infanterie-Regiment Nr. 243, photographed in October 1914. His C96 holster is unconventionally attached to his belt by means of a leather strap. (Brett Butterworth collection)

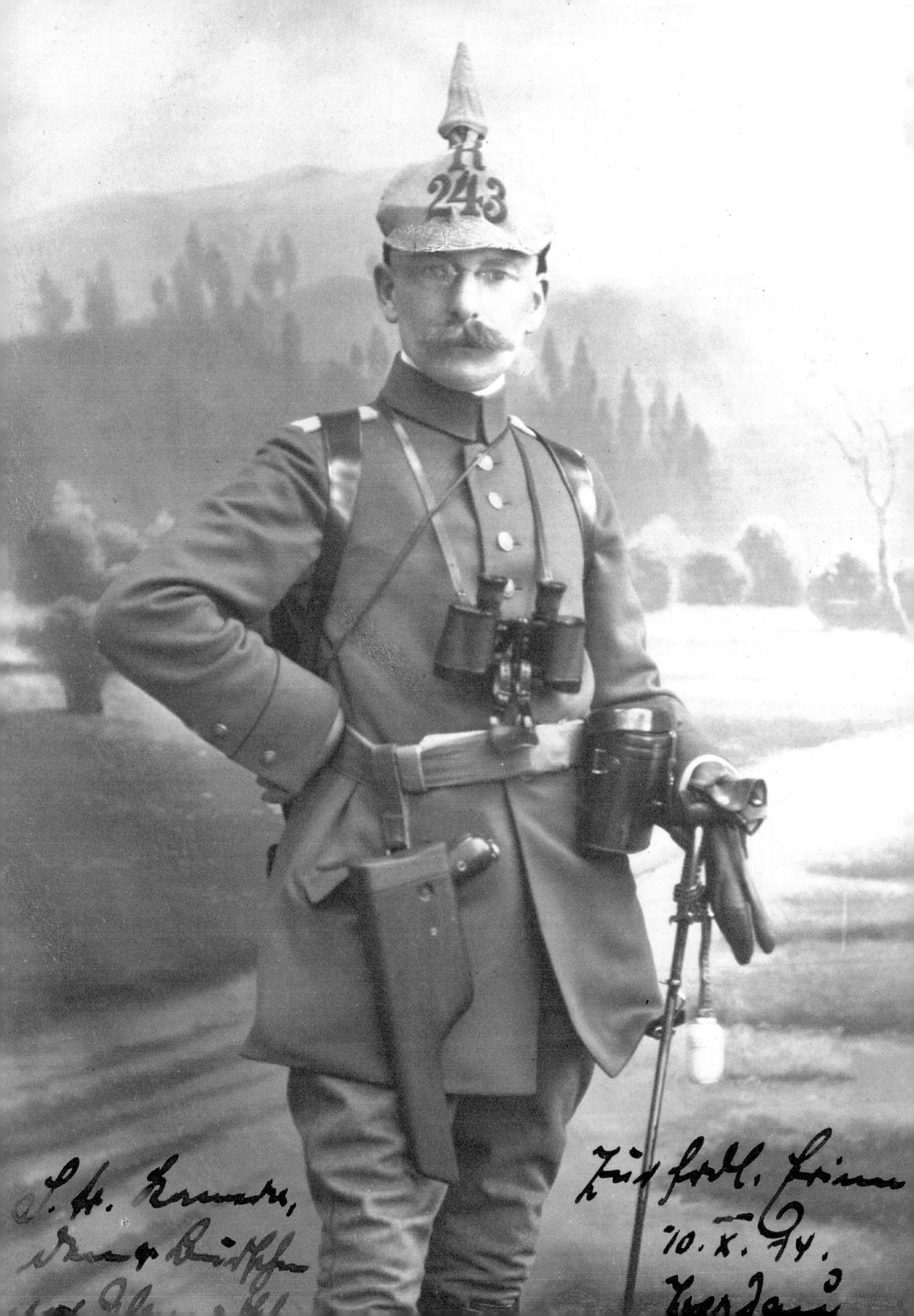
R
243
10. X. 14.

Second fiddle

The C96 fared well in US military trials of 1900 and 1903, though it was disparaged as being 'large and cumbersome' and 'of foreign manufacture' (quoted in Erickson & Pate 1985: 12). Despite the C96 passing all of the required tests, however, the Ordnance Board chose not to proceed with troop trials. Though it is unclear why this was so, the United States was certainly wedded to the perceived 'stopping power' of the .45 calibre, based upon its experience with .38-calibre revolvers during the 1899 Moro Rebellion. 'Luger' pistols purchased for further trial were chambered in the .45 M1906 cartridge that would, along with the Colt pistol, ultimately gain acceptance as the Colt M1911 (.45 ACP).

Though the US government was interested in the potential benefits of modern self-loading firearms, there was a distinct element of 'technophobia' in some of the objections raised to the C96. One piece distributed to US newspapers and periodicals in 1899–1900 bemoaned the role of the Mauser pistol in hastening the decline of the romantic cavalry ideal, complaining that 'In some respects it is a great improvement … but it will inspire no poets. Imagine Tennyson writing the 'Charge of the Light Brigade' about a cavalry regiment armed with Mauser automatics' (Anon 1899b: 4).

Whether as a result of inherent conservatism or the superiority of rival designs, large-scale military success for the C96 did not come until the outbreak of war in 1914 when, realizing the shortfall in sidearms, German authorities permitted officers and NCOs to purchase C96s in the civilian 7.63mm calibre. Many sales were privately made, but significant numbers of C96s were also issued from government arsenals. By 1916 Prussia was forced to consider a substitute standard pistol (*Behelfspistole*) to meet the unprecedented new demand. Having originally rejected the C96, the German military now became Mauser's biggest single customer, ordering 150,000 of which around 130,000 were actually delivered and officially marked as government property for issue to the military. Unlike the pistols already in military use, these were chambered in the existing service-standard 9mm Parabellum cartridge. To prevent users attempting to chamber existing stocks of 7.63mm ammunition, the 9×19mm pistols had a large numeral '9' cut or burned into their grips and usually filled with red paint (hence the nickname 'Red Nine'). These roughly made wartime weapons represent the low point of C96 production quality, but were nevertheless well put together and reliable.

Like the P08 'Luger', the C96 was collected by Allied soldiers and officers as a souvenir. These were not merely war trophies, having a deadly practical purpose as trench weapons *par excellence*. In this the C96 with its two additional shots and standard-issue stock had the edge over the standard P08. It is important to note that C96s were also commercially available in 9×19mm. Indeed, the chambering was an obvious upgrade that did not reduce capacity. Despite this, the original 7.63mm remained the preferred ammunition in China and Russia.

Official US accounts reported the equipment of a typical German assault detachment in 1918 as two MG 08/15 light machine guns and one 'automatic rifle (musket)' (probably the MP 18/I submachine

The 9×19mm Parabellum cartridge (at left) designed for the P08 'Luger' pistol and used in the 'Red Nine' C96. The 7.63×25mm round is shown for comparison purposes. (© Royal Armouries)

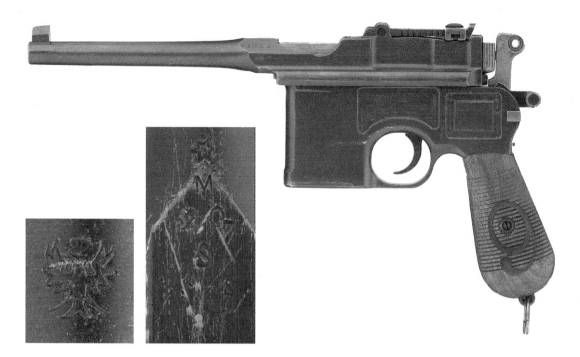

gun, also known as the 'Bergmann Muskete') as fire support. The other soldiers of the detachment each carried a Mauser pistol, a trench knife or bayonet and a complement of 16 stick and eight 'egg' grenades. With only 12,500 submachine guns produced by the end of World War I, stocked Mauser and 'artillery' LP08 Luger pistols continued to be used in the assault until the end of hostilities. Though theoretically inferior to purpose-designed submachine guns, these semi-automatic pistols could be shot very rapidly (350–400rd/min), and were lighter and more compact. In 1917 Mauser even designed a wholly new carbine based upon the C96 with a long, detachable 40-round magazine, hoping to sell it to the German military as a trench weapon. This was an even more expensive design that would have required new tooling, and as such was never mass-produced.

German 'Broomhandles' also saw extensive use in World War II, though by this time natural wastage and the defeat of 1919 had taken their toll on the original inventory. Such was the need for pistols that 1,050 Spanish Astra M900-series pistols were ordered for units of the

A 9mm German military-contract pistol. The Prussian eagle mark on the magazine housing was applied to identify officially procured substitute standard pistols (*Behelfspistolen*) to prevent theft. (© Royal Armouries PR.4101)

Two close-up photographs of an Austrian C96 marked 'I R.11' for Infanterie-Regiment *Johann Georg Prinz von Sachsen* Nr. 11. Germany's wartime ally Austria-Hungary acquired more than 14,000 C96s during World War I, some of which were still in the inventory of the Bundesheer in 1938. (Courtesy of King Rhoton)

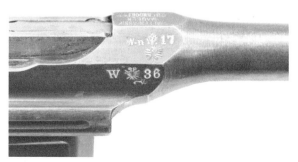

Wehrmacht. These were similar enough to the C96 to simplify training and logistics somewhat and, while not in 9mm Parabellum, were chambered in 7.63mm Mauser, which remained a substitute standard calibre. By this time quantities of the M712 Schnellfeuer machine pistol had also been purchased and went to elements of the Heer (including motorcycle dispatch-riders), Kriegsmarine naval infantry and the Waffen-SS. A significant user was the Luftwaffe, which purchased 7,800 pistols in 1940 for issue to bomber crews, more as an early form of 'personal defence weapon' than with any intent of air-to-air firing (as had been done a generation earlier).

As the ultimate expression of the compact firepower offered by Mauser's original design, the M712 Schnellfeuer gave a final boost to sales of the C96 family when it was released in 1933. Outside of Germany, however, military customers do not seem to have appreciated the need for this rather niche weapon. Yugoslavia conducted trials with the M712 in prototype forms, with a view to equipping specialist mountain and assault units with machine pistols, but the trials revealed a number of mechanical flaws with the prototypes in sustained fire over several thousand rounds. Based upon proposed improvements, the Yugoslav government agreed to purchase 2,000 pistols. Actual deliveries did not take place until 1941, however, apparently due to second thoughts over the very concept of a military machine pistol. It is not known whether the type was ever actually issued. Fully automatic 'Broomhandles' would meet with greater success with law-enforcement personnel and, notably, in China.

A number of Mauser pistols were provided to Nordic countries during the inter-war period, perhaps as a response to the rise of the Soviet Union. Certainly, examples exist with Finnish military markings along with photographic evidence of their use. Here, a Mauser-armed Finnish soldier takes a prisoner during World War II. His method of holding the pistol with bent elbow is typical of the C96 era. (Tom Laemlein / Armor Plate Press)

The 'Box Cannon'

China's defeat in the First Sino-Japanese War (1894–95) led to concerted efforts to re-equip its armed forces. The Chinese government turned to Germany, notably purchasing tooling from Mauser to make M1888 'Commission' rifles at the Hanyang Arsenal. This was followed by purchases of other weapons over the next few decades, including Mauser pistols; in the main these were of German military surplus and wartime 'standard commercial' pistols, as well as early and late post-war 'Bolo' models. These were later joined by quantities of M1930 and M712 models. In total, some 300,000 were imported between 1916 and 1936, making China the biggest single adopter of C96-pattern pistols. Some were German war surplus, but most were new. These were supplemented by numbers of Spanish copies and derivatives (see page 60). Extensive unlicensed copying also took place, both officially at government arsenals, and illicitly in small workshops. This resulted in a unique and prolific range of C96 variants and derivatives in China.

Official military users and warlord-controlled fighters alike favoured semi-automatic pistols of various types, partly because pistols were exempt from the arms embargo placed on China in 1919. The C96, with its detachable shoulder stock, was therefore supposedly popular as a rifle or carbine stand-in. This embargo lasted only for ten years and applied only to signatory nations, however, meaning that rifles and automatic weapons could be, and were, imported (for example from Brno in Czechoslovakia). The Chinese cultural preference for the Mauser-pattern pistol therefore seems to be the main reason for its proliferation there.

The early imported pistols began to appear in actual use almost as soon as they arrived. A newspaper report from January 1916 describes the detention and search in Shanghai of the Chinese steamer *Kobe Maru*. Two men were arrested and a wooden trunk recovered. The trunk was found to have 'a false bottom containing 100 sticks of dynamite, one Mauser pistol and 90 rounds of ammunition' (Anon 1916: 8). The old Chinese Empire had fallen in 1911, and numerous warlords rose during the following years to fill the resulting power vacuum. This coincided

OVERLEAF

Marshal Sun Chuanfang's pistol section photographed at Jaixing in early 1927, only months before Sun's defeat at the hands of Chinese government forces. (Photo by Topical Press Agency/ Hulton Archive/Getty Images)

A rough 'craft-produced' copy of the C96. (Courtesy of King Rhoton)

41

A high-quality copy of the C96 made at the Shansei arsenal. (Courtesy of King Rhoton)

with increasing availability of imported C96s and emerging production of local copies. These men were known for their personal use and military issue of these weapons. Marshal Sun Chuanfang even maintained a specific unit of soldiers armed exclusively with the C96. By the mid-1920s, Sun was able to capture a large area of eastern China despite efforts by the Chinese government to wrest control from the independent warlords in a campaign known as the Northern Expedition. Sun's army was eventually destroyed in spring 1927 and he was forced to flee. The Chinese Civil War began that same year as tensions reached a high between the governing Nationalist Kuomintang party and the Chinese Communist party. This would only serve to increase demand for C96-pattern pistols, and they would see use by both sides throughout the war.

The high demand for firearms in China, especially pistols, was in large part responsible for the Spanish versions of the C96 that began to be imported in the late 1920s (see page 60). These were not exclusively intended for the Chinese market, but China was certainly the biggest customer and it is unlikely that either Mauser or its Spanish rivals would have put fully automatic variants into production without Chinese influence. Just as local craftsmen today produce weapons inspired by the Kalashnikov rifle (and in a few cases, even the C96) for those who cannot afford the real thing, at this time demand led to a surge in Chinese 'craft production'. As with more recent workshop firearms, the metals and methods used were often substandard and resulted in unsafe, inaccurate

The 'Box Cannon' unleashed (opposite)

Selective-fire pistols are practical only at extremely close range. Here, a desperate soldier of the National Revolutionary Army empties his M712 Schnellfeuer at a Communist Party of China guerrilla conducting a house-to-house sweep in Taiyuan, c.1948. At this stage of the Chinese Civil War, Nationalist Kuomintang government forces were on the verge of defeat at the hands of the insurgent Communists. The Communist fighter also holds a 'Broomhandle' variant in the form of a locally made Shanxi Type 17 pistol in .45 ACP.

weapons. Markings were either spurious or missing entirely. Some of the Chinese attempts were close copies of the original, however, and appear to be at least somewhat serviceable, if a far cry from the products coming out of Oberndorf. Those produced at Shansei and Peking-Tianjin arsenals are particularly good. Hanyang, Taku and Taiyuan arsenals also created their own specific evolutions of the design, Hanyang being the most prolific Chinese maker of the type. Production overall is impossible to quantify, but reached the tens of thousands.

The only .45-calibre C96-pattern pistols produced were made in China, which had a surplus of the big cartridge having been in receipt of military aid from the United States. The 'Broomhandles' that found their way to the Koninklijk Nederlands Indisch Leger (KNIL or 'Royal Netherlands East Indies Army') in World War II are likely to have been sourced from (or via) China. These were introduced in 1941 as the 'Pistool M.', joining a wide assortment of small arms obtained by the Dutch government-in-exile from any source willing to supply them, as the colony faced invasion from Imperial Japan.

EFFECTIVENESS

Reliability

The Mauser pistol earned a reputation as an effective weapon, safety issues notwithstanding. There is no doubt that it was a quick-firing pistol with a high capacity, but it is important to assess objectively historical claims regarding its capability. As with all early self-loading firearms, especially pistols, many believed that the Mauser was prone to jamming. Second Lieutenant Anson of The East Surrey Regiment thought it 'Liable to jam through bad feeding. Would not like to depend on it after a sandstorm' (WO Paper 7101/B/6401). Similar complaints damned the Mauser in British trials conducted in 1901. The Chief Inspector of Small Arms reported 55 stoppages out of 180 rounds, attributed to a weak magazine spring. Only four failures in 180 rounds were experienced when fired with the stock. This poor performance is surprising, but might be explained by weak springs and/or inappropriate ammunition choice (for example if underpowered Borchardt cartridges were used). Another report issued that same year from the Royal Navy shore establishment HMS *Excellent* was even more damning: 'Advantages: Nil. Disadvantages - Perpetual jams. Bad feed. Unsafe. Pistol when loaded and cocked will fire when the safety is moved from "safe" to "fire" (without touching the trigger or hammer)' (WO Paper 77/19/1459). Attempts by the author to reproduce this suggest that it can only have been the result of incorrect reassembly (placing the sear spring in the wrong position). Until remedied, this would also prevent the weapon from firing, which might explain some of the stoppages experienced.

As to complaints in service, it is possible that some users, used to the simpler revolver, did not appreciate the additional care and maintenance required for early self-loading pistols in general. Regardless, this was far

The holster-stock

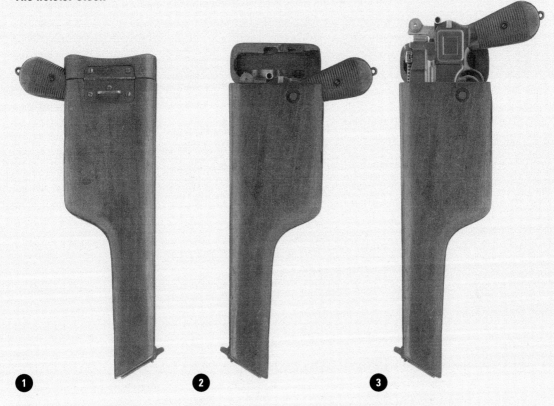

1 **2** **3**

One of the most celebrated features of the C96 was its dual-purpose detachable wooden case/holster and shoulder stock (*Anschlagkasten*), which could be attached when needed for more accurate fire. (This idea was nothing new; the C93 Borchardt pistol had been supplied with a wooden paddle stock with a leather holster attached to it.) Each stock was hand-fitted to an individual weapon and until the M1930 was even marked with the latter's serial number due to a lack of interchangeability. Even then, there was always some lateral 'play' that could affect accuracy. Nevertheless, it was a useful option for many buyers, not least the German military. This sequence of images shows the simple and fairly rapid process by which the pistol could be drawn and turned into a pistol carbine of sorts.

Securely fastened into the holster-stock (**1**), the pistol is safe from knocks, scrapes and adverse weather. A suspension loop is built into the hinge. A chequered button is depressed and the lid hinged open to reveal the weapon (**2**). This action is far slower than simply opening the flap of a leather holster, and is the weakest point of this arrangement. The pistol begins to clear the holster (**3**), after which the lid must be firmly flipped shut, as it will act as the butt-plate of the stock. The holster-stock is flipped upside down and the metal catch aligned with the slot in the grip of the pistol (**4**). It clicks firmly into place when slid upwards. (© Royal Armouries PR.11417)

4

from the universal experience. Winston Churchill reported that 'the weapon did not get out of order in a country where the desert sand affects all machinery' (Churchill 1902: 351). Field stripping for cleaning is straightforward by comparison with period rivals, although the supplied *Putzstock* tool/cleaning rod (or an appropriate screwdriver) is required to remove the bolt. Available period information is admittedly limited (in English, at any rate), but the experience of the modern collector and limited testing by the author suggests that the C96 was at least as reliable as most contemporary designs. This includes the 'Luger', but not the Colt M1911, which set a new benchmark for reliable and effective handguns.

Accuracy

Informal experimentation by the author confirms that the C96 is no less accurate off-hand than a modern pistol at typical combat ranges (*c*.10m), regardless of long- or short-barrel patterns. The large V-notch sights are also superior to those of many period rivals. The distinctive grip is not as uncomfortable as it might appear, although the shooter can suffer 'hammer bite' with a modern high grasp. Perceived recoil is not severe, but the top-heavy design does produce significant muzzle rise that compromises precise rapid fire. The substantial overall weight is also a factor with prolonged use. The shoulder stock greatly increases effective range up to at least 100m for an average shot. Modern tests have shown that it is, in fact, possible to hit a man-sized target at 300m if using the stock and firing from the prone position. Here, the astonishingly long ranges marked on the typical C96 rear sight deserve special attention. The sight is marked from 50m, regarded today as the maximum effective range of a service pistol (at the time a *minimum* requirement in many trials), up to 300m, 500m and even 1,000m on many sights. This was due in large part to the universal supply of the wooden holster-stock, which was actually believed to allow for effective (if not truly accurate) fire out to these ranges.

Importantly, in 1896 the pistol was primarily a cavalry weapon. A relatively low-velocity pistol bullet might arrive only approximately in the area of the intended target with most of its energy spent, but this kind of high-angle 'plunging' fire was used to harass, disorder or suppress enemy formations. In other words, such long-range fire was only minimally effective, but did have a theoretical application for cavalry operating in open terrain such as that found in British colonies overseas. Equally, artillery crews and military users not normally issued a rifle or carbine would at least have the ability to project fire out to long range. It is notable, however, that some C96s retailed by Westley Richards were refitted with modified sights for 300m, and German military 9mm pistols were produced with 500m sights. Numerous contemporary sources support the range potential of the weapon. Churchill believed it effective out to 800 yards (732m). Lieutenant-Colonel Mills of 1st Battalion, The Royal Dublin Fusiliers believed it to be 'accurate up to 500 yards with the shoulder stock' (WO Paper 7101/B/5733). There is good reason to be sceptical of these claims, however, as neither man had fired the weapon in combat at such ranges. There is some truth to these outlandish claims, though. Colonial warfare taking place in wide, open spaces would have afforded some limited opportunity for long-range fire. A group of cavalry or an officer assisting his rifle-armed men might reach out to longer ranges in rapid, plunging volley fire. Here, the objective (assuming no machine gun was available) was to disorder, suppress or simply to demoralize the enemy, not to strike individual men with precision shots. Incidences of this would have been rare, however, as anyone with the need to fire out to 500 yards (457m) was issued a carbine or rifle for that purpose. Historical evidence for this comes from none other than T.E. Lawrence, who wrote to his family regarding an encounter he had with a would-be robber soon after arrival in Syria in 1909:

> he put in a shot at about 200 yards, which I was able to return rather successfully: for his horse promptly bolted about half a mile ... he stopped about 800 yards away to contemplate the scenery, and wonder how on earth a person with nothing but a pistol could shoot so far: and when I put up my sights as high as they would go and plumped a bullet somewhere over his nut he made off like a steeple-chaser. (Quoted in Garnett 1939: 79)

While selective-fire variants of the C96 were popular, especially in China and Spain, their practical value is highly questionable. Most operate at around 1,100rd/min, making them quite uncontrollable without the shoulder stock (the Astra Model F is an exception; see page 62). Experiments conducted by the author with an M712 Schnellfeuer show that at very close range (1–3m) it is possible to give effective one-handed defensive fire (all three shots on a 210×297mm target). By canting the weapon sharply to one side, as it is rumoured was done by Chinese users, the cumulative recoil may be turned to the firer's advantage, drawing a line of fire across the target. With the stock fitted, short bursts (themselves not easy to pull off without practice) *may* be contained within the same target area at 15m. Given that group sizes will double proportionately with distance, however, it might prove difficult at twice this distance to hit an enemy at all. By far the best use of a weapon like the Schnellfeuer would be as the German infantry employed it; with stock fitted, as a substitute for a fully fledged submachine gun in trench or urban warfare. In almost all other situations, semi-automatic fire would be more effective.

A fine view of a 7.63mm C96 in the hands of a *Kanonier* (gunner) of 4. Württembergisches Feld-Artillerie-Regiment Nr. 65. (Courtesy of Sam Wouters)

'Stopping power'

Another important consideration was the nebulous concept of so-called 'stopping power'. In an era when this power was believed to derive from the 'shock' effect of a big, heavy bullet striking the enemy's body, many felt that the relatively small and lightweight Mauser bullet was insufficient for 'savage warfare'. An article in *Country Life* magazine explains:

> Nickel-plated bullets, such as are used in the magazine pistols, are not well suited, say their opponents, for stopping a rush by the enemy; the bullets go whistling through the bodies of those hit by them without

doing them very much damage, certainly not enough to stop their on-rush effectually. At Omdurman, for instance, one officer of the Lancers is said to have dropped three Dervishes dead with three discharges of his Webley revolver, while his companion who was armed with a Mauser pistol fired ten shots into as many Dervishes, but did not succeed in dropping or even stopping a single one of them. If true, the story tells well in favour of the present Service revolver at close quarters. (Anon 1899a: 264)

The phrase 'whistling through' was used advisedly, as informal testing carried out by the Sporting Goods Review showed that the normal 7.63mm bullet would pass through a side of beef 1ft (30.5cm) thick, with penetration to spare; but they, too, commented on the 'clean' holes that it bored. One of the British officers responding to an official request for opinions on the type described the weapon's 'man-stopping power' as 'defective' by comparison with the .455 Webley revolver. The science of the day, though underdeveloped in this area, appeared to support these claims. Experiments carried out in 1897 by the German surgeon Paul von Bruns showed impressive penetration. However, at ranges between 20m and 200m small, 'clean' wounds were observed in animal tissue. In one heated exchange of letters involving distributor Westley Richards, it was claimed that the weapon might not even incapacitate a rabbit! Nor was this an exclusively 'Western' belief. The Russians and Chinese may have set stock by the 7.63mm bullet, but British folklorist Mary Edith Durham reported in 1909 that some Albanian fighters believed the Mauser bullet to be outright harmless, to the extent of proposing a demonstration in which she would shoot one of them through the hand! Others did not feel as strongly, however, and a photograph from the Imperial War Museums archive shows another Albanian militiaman proudly displaying his Mauser.

Some tests – admittedly less than scientific but quite plausible – suggested one Mauser bullet could kill three men if they stood in a line. One officer reported having killed a horse at 400 yards (366m)! In fact, the weapon would go on to earn a reputation as an exceptionally powerful pistol in countries such as China and Ireland. How was it that the same weapon could polarize opinion in this way? The answer lies in the true strengths and weaknesses of 7.63×25mm ammunition. It offered very high velocity for its day, and could easily penetrate to a lethal depth even through layers of clothing or equipment, at extended range, or when fired at an oblique angle. As with the early round-nosed 6–7mm rifle bullets of the era, if the 7.63mm bullet struck bone it might shatter it, causing far worse wounds than otherwise. William Fairbairn reported on just such an incident with the use of the word 'pulped' in his book *Shooting to Live* (Fairbairn & Sykes 1987: 75). A .30-calibre pistol bullet is also small in size, however – too small for modern self-defence use. Modern research shows that fully jacketed pistol bullets, regardless of velocity and mass, create wound channels in soft tissue only as large in diameter as the bullet itself. This limits tissue damage and blood loss. Period complaints therefore reflect the inconsistent performance of this type of ammunition. One shot might fail to stop a motivated assailant; the next might hit

Expanding ammunition from Westley Richards: the flat-nosed 'All-Range' bullet (above) and the more aerodynamic 'capped' version (below). From *Modern Sporting Gunnery*, 1906. (University of Toronto Libraries Collection)

something vital and result in incapacitation. This is borne out by first-hand accounts of the effects of the Mauser's bullet on the human body. Notably, a Captain Ionides of 1st Battalion, The East Surrey Regiment shot two Boer fighters with his C96 on different occasions with just such differing results. The first incident seems to support detractors of the cartridge, as he hit at a range of 25yd (23m), the 'bullet hitting small of back and ran up to his neck; wound was not dangerous'; in the second incident he 'shot a Boer retiring at 50 yards range. Boer fell into river, body not recovered' (WO Paper 7101/B/6401).

As early as 1899, alternative bullet types were available for the C96 including those with flat, soft or hollow noses. Winston Churchill recounts having two chargers of 'soft-point' ammunition on his person in Natal in 1899. Worried that his Boer captors might not take kindly to the idea of him using controversial 'Dum-Dum' ammunition on their comrades, he managed to get rid of the offending rounds. These early bullets did not expand well at pistol velocities, and the degree to which they might make up for any deficiency in terminal effect is questionable. Flat-nosed or 'wadcutter' bullets were (and remain) even less potent. Still, these efforts clearly show the strength of feeling regarding the shortcomings of 7.63mm ammunition. Reflecting widely held views at the time regarding the ability of 'savages' to shrug off certain bullets, one British officer recommended that; 'If the Mauser is adopted the solid bullet should be used for civilised, and the blunt nose for uncivilised warfare' ('Reports on Equipment in S. Africa'). In contrast, Captain Marshall of 4th Battalion, The Cheshire Regiment did not think 'lightness and smallness of bullet a great disadvantage especially in civilised warfare, and any deficiency in man-stopping power is counterbalanced by increased range, accuracy and rapidity of fire' (WO Paper 7101/B/6401). By the first years of the 20th century, Westley Richards had developed two new expanding bullets that did expand reliably in tissue. According to one account, the soft-nose and metal-capped soft-nosed Westley Richards designs allowed the bullet to expand to three times its original size, making it far more effective. No self-loading pistol or ammunition was to see official British adoption until the 9mm Parabellum Browning Hi-Power pistol, some 40 years later.

THE ADVENTURER'S COMPANION

It may not have fired the biggest bullet on the proverbial block, but unlike other self-loaders the Mauser did find favour in the hunting and sporting world. The specifically designed carbine was a commercial failure, but some hunters, fishermen and outdoorsmen carried the pistol as a sidearm for use against wild animals or even as a primary weapon, from the North American wilderness to the Himalayas. Either the 7.63mm or 9mm versions would penetrate the thick skull of a bear far better than a shot from the revolvers available prior to World War II, as trapper and guide Adam Moorse discovered, using the weapon to despatch the bears that he trapped. One Canadian hunter was able to bring down a bull moose with a 7.63mm C96, and British journalist Arthur Moore wrote of shooting down an attacking eagle with his pistol. Some thought enough of the gun as a hunting tool to recommend getting a gunsmith to install a telescopic sight.

Overseas travellers and adventurers in the early years of the 20th century often packed a Mauser. It could be carried almost anywhere, and used to hunt or to protect life, property and limb from dangerous animals or indeed criminals (just as it might be used by criminals). As noted earlier, T.E. Lawrence chose a 'Broomhandle' as his sidearm on his archaeological adventures, albeit with mixed results. But the big handgun often did prove its worth when far from home. With assistance from two other men armed with a revolver and a shotgun, globetrotting British gold-miner Herbert Way was, with his Mauser, able to resist and even capture a crew of Chinese pirates who attacked his boat as it left Shanghai. Admittedly the pirates were armed only with clubs! Explorer A. Loton Ridger carried a C96 as a survival tool in Africa, while Spanish–American War correspondent (later war artist and cartoonist) John T. McCutcheon kept the Mauser pistol he had carried on his travels abroad as a sentimental souvenir. Pioneering motorist adventurers Bede Bentley and Clifford Hallé included one in their inventory for their 1,000km drive from Djibouti to Addis Ababa to deliver a car to the Abyssinian emperor, Menelik II. In her travels east to Mongolia, Mary Beatrix Nunns (aka 'Beatrix Bulstrode') took time to practise with a C96 that she concealed under her Burberry coat.

Westerners abroad noted the amazement with which indigenous peoples regarded the Mauser. In parts of the world where the bolt-action rifle was not yet known, this is hardly surprising. The C96 belonging to noted explorer and big-game hunter Walter D.M. Bell was apparently greatly respected by local people in what is now Uganda, who dubbed it 'Bom-Bom' and thought it 'equal to a hundred ordinary rifles' (Bell 1923: 23). Bell also wrote of frightening away those who threatened life or property by landing repeated shots in the sand near them at ranges up to hundreds of metres away. Not all opponents were so ignorant of modern technology, however, and by 1906 the 'Broomhandle' might be found as far afield as North Africa. In that year Major John Boyes, a British adventurer, decided to make a present of his own C96 to Emperor Menelik II, only for the unimpressed Abyssinian ruler to show him two examples that he obtained himself. Fortunately, Boyes noticed that the man had an eye complaint, and instead won him over with the off-the-cuff gift of a simple pair of goggles.

TAKING TO THE SKIES

As they typically held officer rank, pilots on all sides in World War I carried sidearms. Before true fighter aircraft armed with machine guns were developed, these weapons might actually be used to attack enemy aircraft and aircrew, though it was extremely difficult to score a hit on a moving target from an aircraft that was itself manoeuvring violently in three-dimensional space. Although bolt-action service rifles were used,

self-loading and automatic firearms offered real advantages despite their greater complexity. With the ability to fire rapidly without disrupting the shooting position or hold, it was possible to create a controlled but dispersed pattern of bullets, increasing the probability of hitting something vital. Rifles of this type were rare, however, so many pilots and observers carried double-action revolvers. Of those available, therefore, the C96 was a logical choice. Major John F.A. Higgins of No. 5 Squadron, Royal Flying Corps (RFC) actually had his Mauser's holster mounted to the side of the cockpit of his Bristol Scout to allow for a quick draw once his fuselage-mounted Lee-Enfield rifle had run dry.

Though something of a default option prior to the adaptation of machine guns to air service, the C96 made an excellent back-up weapon in the event of a machine-gun stoppage or lack of ammunition. Flyers of various countries carried them. Austro-Hungarian and Italian aircrew had access to the issue variants of their respective militaries, but many others purchased theirs privately. Notably, the famous French ace Lieutenant Jean Navarre attacked an Aviatik B.I on 1 April 1915, his observer opening fire with his C96. In Britain the weapon became pseudo-official when it was specifically recommended for use by RFC aircrew in an official document entitled 'Method of attack of hostile aeroplane during combat'. This was produced by the General Headquarters in 1916, well

Royal Flying Corps Bristol Scout 633 or 648, Western Front 1914 or 1915. A stockless SMLE rifle and C96 pistol in leather holster are mounted by means of metal brackets, as well as a rack of rifle grenades with fabric streamer stabilizers for use as bombs. (RAF Museum X003-2602/2796, © Trustees of the Royal Air Force Museum)

after machine guns had been proven as air-service weapons, and specified that pilots and observers should carry pistols and specifically recommended Mausers. There may have been an element of tradition here; after all, the pilot was often seen as the spiritual successor to the cavalryman, the 'knight of the sky'. The primary motivation was as a practical secondary weapon, however, for resorting to a loaded pistol was sometimes preferable to mid-air efforts to clear a Lewis or Vickers gun stoppage. *The Aeroplane* noted in 1917 an incident in which an observer with a jammed machine gun was able to make a 'kill' with a Mauser automatic pistol. In another combat that took place in July 1915, Captain John A. Liddell of No. 7 Squadron, RFC was flying an RE5 biplane on his first reconnaissance flight since arriving in Saint-Omer, France. Liddell was forced to draw his Mauser when his Lewis gun jammed. He was not able to make either weapon count, however, and returned to base with a number of bullet holes in his aircraft.

German aircrew too equipped themselves with C96s. Indeed, the type featured in one of the first-ever aerial dogfights. This took place over northern France in August 1914 and is claimed as the first RFC 'kill' of the war. Lieutenant Cuthbert Euan Rabagliati of The King's Own (Yorkshire Light Infantry) and RFC was flying as an observer in an Avro 504 biplane of No. 5 Squadron piloted by Second Lieutenant Charles W. Wilson. Typically thus far in the air war, enemy aircraft had chosen to break contact, but in this case a lone German Etrich Taube monoplane opted to engage. As both aircraft involved were unarmed scouts, an exchange of small-arms fire took place. In Rabagliati's own words:

> We flew around each other for a very long time, the German using a Mauser pistol with a stock set on his shoulder, and I had a .303 army rifle. I fired over a hundred rounds and he did the same with his pistol. On one occasion, he clipped the lobe of my ear and made it bleed which made me very angry but eventually we made a hole in the sump of his engine and all the oil ran out and his engine seized so that he landed at the edge of the Forêt de Mormal, and our cavalry picked him and his observer up and made them prisoners. (IWM Sound Archive 23151)

The semi-automatic Mauser pistol might have afforded the edge here, but in the event it was the sheer power of the Enfield rifle that ended the fight. Rabagliati was later awarded the Military Cross and the Air Force Cross. He rose to the rank of lieutenant-colonel, and after the war became a senior MI6 official.

LAW ENFORCEMENT

The C96 and M712 Schnellfeuer saw use with security forces and police around the world, although neither weapon was a runaway success. Probably the biggest user in this sphere was Germany, notably the Freikorps of the 1920s, the Reichs Finanz Verwaltung (Reich Finance

A Rio de Janeiro military policeman with anti-riot helmet and 'Mod-2' PASAM submachine gun. C96-pattern pistols were also sold to police in South America, with Argentina and Brazil both known users. It is known that the Policia Militar in the state of Rio de Janeiro procured 500 Mauser Schnellfeuers in the 1930s, as these were still in their armoury as late as the 1980s. They were known as the PASAM, or 'Pistola Automatica e Semi-Automatica Mauser'. In the 1970s, 190 of these weapons were modified to make them more practical for what was effectively an urban combat role. Two variants were made, both adding a barrel shroud, Tommy gun-style front grip, and a fixed tubular stock. These additions converted the machine pistol into a fully fledged submachine gun, although a lack of 20-round magazines would seriously limit capability. These modified weapons were essentially a stopgap measure and were replaced by the 1990s. (Courtesy of Ronaldo Olive)

Administration) and various state and local police forces. The World War II-era *Zollgrenzschutz* customs and border police also received the type. Pre-war Russian police carried their 7.63mm pistols in their wooden holster-stocks even when on traffic duty, as one Canadian visitor noted. Spanish policemen made extensive use of the pattern, albeit in the form of the locally made fully automatic derivatives. If this seems surprising today, it must be remembered that Spain was beset by civil unrest and conflict in the inter-war years. At least 1,350 Astra M901 and M902 machine pistols (7.63×25mm) were confiscated and issued to a newly formed unit of *Guardia de Asalto* ('assault guards'). A pistol-sized personal weapon with an optional stock and full-automatic capability made sense for these specialist riot and urban pacification police. The Astra Model F was specifically designed for sale to the Guardia Civil, but was chambered in the more powerful military 9mm Largo cartridge. This was successful in trials, resulting in a purchase in 1934 of 1,000 of these machine pistols (see page 62). Most of these (950) were delivered before the outbreak of the Spanish Civil War in July 1936. As 1,126 were produced in total,

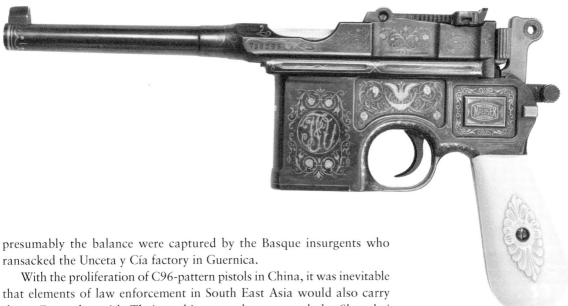

A beautifully decorated Argentine example of a 'transitional' M1930. (Courtesy of King Rhoton)

presumably the balance were captured by the Basque insurgents who ransacked the Unceta y Cía factory in Guernica.

With the proliferation of C96-pattern pistols in China, it was inevitable that elements of law enforcement in South East Asia would also carry them. Examples with Thai markings are known, and the Shanghai Municipal Police (SMP; see below) who preferred Colt self-loading pistols nevertheless held Mauser examples in their armoury. These were not simply examples captured from criminals, but actually saw use. In one celebrated incident in 1929, Detective Richard Moir of the SMP engaged seven armed kidnappers alone, killing five with the two Mauser pistols he carried, and arresting two. Moir had delivered 27 of the 37 shots fired and thanks to his issue steel vest and handheld shield, escaped with only a 'slight wound in the left shoulder' (Anon 1929: 2). This use of the Mauser pistol as an equalizer against greater numbers had parallels in military action. In his 1901 Second Anglo-Boer War memoir, Lieutenant-Colonel St John Corbet Gore (also a C96 user) wrote of an emergency ambush initiated near Elandslaagte by a fellow officer: 'Two Boers must have heard something. They were mounted, and rode straight towards where Reynolds was lying. He let them come close up, and then said in a low voice, "Hands up!" "Ja!" said the Dutchmen, beginning to dismount with their rifles to shoot. Then Reynolds let them have it – right and left with his Mauser pistol' (Gore 1901: 146).

Though the Mauser pistol had some success in law-enforcement circles, it was for the most part displaced by double-action revolvers. To police buyers with limited budgets these represented an intuitive upgrade to existing single-action types, whereas the Mauser was an expensive leap into the unknown. Even though a police weapon might not suffer the abuse that its military counterpart would in the field, by the same token police did not necessarily require a large, heavy and powerful full-size service pistol. Attitudes in this respect changed over the years, but not soon enough to encourage wider adoption of the Mauser in favour of later, more capable designs. With a dearth of large military and police contracts, the Mauser pistol was fated to become the favoured sidearm of revolutionaries, paramilitaries and common criminals.

59

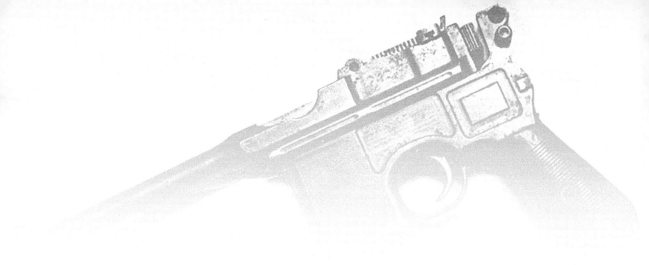

IMPACT
A legendary weapon

THE SINCEREST FORM OF FLATTERY

As we have seen, the original Mauser C96 'Broomhandle' was one of the most successful weapons of its class ever produced, seeing documented ownership and use around the world. Importantly, it also inspired a range of imitators. The success of the C96 in China inspired the expanding Spanish firearms industry to enter that lucrative market, but at a lower price point. The first company to exploit Mauser's design in this way was Beístegui Hermanos, which in 1927 applied for a Spanish patent to protect a new range of 'Royal' pistols. These were virtually direct copies of the original, built to a lower price and completely unlicensed. Another range was dubbed the 'Azul', apparently produced by Eulogio Arostegui, which seems to have been the first to incorporate a detachable box magazine. Mauser records show that the firm had investigated the idea of a detachable magazine as early as 1910, but it is thought that Paul Mauser's affinity for the fixed magazine prevented this from being put into production until the 1930s.

The mysteriously named 'ETAI' machine pistol was a reverse-engineered copy of the Mauser M1930, appearing later that same year. It incorporated significant internal differences intended to reduce production costs, primarily a simplified lock frame. This was further redesigned to incorporate an automatic sear, creating the 'Royal MM31' (1931) on which the selector switch was placed on the right-hand side, thus preventing accidental movement. Four iterations were produced, the first two being charger-fed in ten- and 20-shot forms whereas the latter two accepted detachable magazines. Proprietary 30-round magazines were produced for the third model, while the final variant was specifically redesigned to accept the smaller ten- or 20-round Mauser M712 magazines. This hints at the greater market success of the German

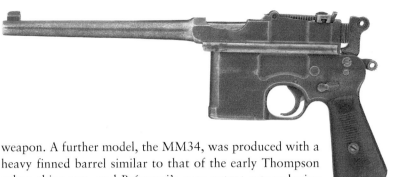

The Beístegui Hermanos 'ETAI' machine pistol, with selector switch on the left side. (© Royal Armouries PR.8649)

weapon. A further model, the MM34, was produced with a heavy finned barrel similar to that of the early Thompson submachine gun, and Beístegui's own patent rate-reducing gear in the grip. At this point the weapon was practically a submachine gun with a detachable stock, although for some reason it retained a ten- or 20-round fixed (rather than detachable) magazine.

Rival company Unceta y Cía also produced 'Broomhandles' under their brand name 'Astra' from 1927. These were substantially redesigned by comparison with the Royal range. The first model produced was the M900, awarded a Spanish patent on 12 July 1928. This was identical from the operator's point of view to the original C96, being a 7.63mm, charger-fed, semi-automatic pistol with a ten-round capacity. The external design was substantially unchanged, although the extension was 'beefed up' to cope with the more powerful 9×23mm Largo cartridge. The lockwork entirely abandoned the hollowed-out pistol frame and separate lock frame. Instead, in an approach closer to traditional revolver designs, components were fitted directly into the frame and protected by a sliding sideplate, the whole being held together by just two transverse square pegs. Given that there was no imperative to avoid Mauser's patents, this was done for ease of production and also maintenance by owners and gunsmiths more used to working on revolvers and rifles. For the observer, it means that Astra 'Broomhandles' are easily identified (aside from their markings) by the large sliding sideplate on the left side and the bright steel disassembly peg visible on both sides. The downside to the more solid frame was increased weight – 150g more than the original C96 (1.27kg

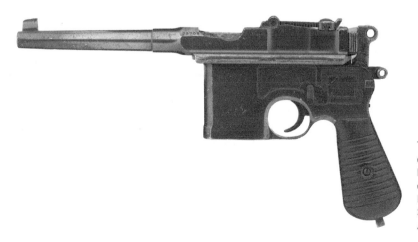

The 'Royal MM31' is a close external copy of the Mauser M1930. The internal mechanism differs from that of both the M1930 and the M712 Schnellfeuer, however. (© Royal Armouries PR.10575)

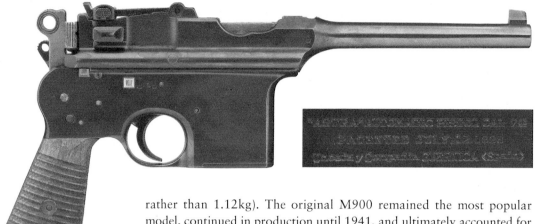

The Spanish Unceta Astra M900. This example is part of the 1943 contract for the German Wehrmacht. (© Royal Armouries PR.4104)

rather than 1.12kg). The original M900 remained the most popular model, continued in production until 1941, and ultimately accounted for over half of all 900-series pistols produced by Unceta y Cía.

All subsequent Astra models were selective fire, starting with the M901, which was essentially an adapted M900 and was therefore saddled with a maximum ten-round capacity. The M902, which also entered production in 1928, added a 20-round internal magazine and a longer barrel – both features likely intended to make the weapon more practical when fitted with its holster-stock, although limited numbers of semi-automatics were also made. In pistol mode, however, it made for an even larger and heftier weapon than the C96 or M712.

The M903 of 1932 reverted to a shorter barrel (though still 20mm longer than the Mauser version, at 160mm) and was modified to accept detachable magazines of ten or 20 rounds. In other words, it mirrored the Nickl-pattern Mauser Schnellfeuer that had arrived on the market in the preceding year. The simple pivoting selector lever on the right side was retained, however, now being marked '1' and '20' for semi- and full-automatic positions. The M903 was also offered in a wider range of chamberings than the Schnellfeuer, being available in 7.63mm Mauser, 9mm Parabellum, .38 Super and 9mm Largo. The classic 7.63mm version would sell well in China and elsewhere, while the remainder kept export options open. In the early 1950s, it would also become the last factory-produced 'Broomhandle' ever made, years after production had ended at the Guernica plant, and decades after Mauser had thrown in the towel. This is because the final 581 examples of the 'Model 903', including 33 semi-automatic only sub-variants, were actually hybrids built using surplus unfinished Model F components. For this reason they were sold as 'Model E'. The final example was sold in 1961.

The Model 904 of 1934 featured an innovative rate reducer built into the grip in an effort to produce a truly practical machine pistol for military and police use. By connecting the hammer to a sprung flywheel via a toothed gear and a linkage rod, the hammer's fall was delayed and the cyclic rate dropped from over 900rd/min to a positively tame 200–350rd/min. This was certainly controllable, but somewhat redundant, as a trained shooter could achieve this rate with a semi-automatic weapon simply using their trigger finger. This patent Unceta rate-reducing mechanism was incorporated into the subsequent Model F for the

Guardia Civil. This was specified in 9mm Largo, then a standard-issue cartridge due to military adoption of the Bergmann 'Mars' pistol in 1903. The selector switch differed slightly in arrangement due to the presence of the rate reducer, and featured yet another different set of markings; 'T' for '*Tiro a tiro*' ('shot by shot') and 'A' for '*ametralladora*' ('machine gun'). Inconveniently for quick operation, the selector switch remained on the right side of the weapon. This compares unfavourably with the improved 1932 version of the German Schnellfeuer, the left-side selector switch of which is, even with its safety button, much quicker to operate and just as safe.

Despite the fact that the first 'Broomhandle' machine pistol was a German and not a Spanish creation, the Spanish equivalents are not direct copies. All of the Spanish derivatives are internally very different from the Schnellfeuer and from each other. In fact, this whole 'extended family' of pistols share surprisingly few details overall, even if (from a user's point of view) they are all similar in size, shape and effectiveness. The important thing for the customer was that the look and heft were right; that the 'spirit' of the 'Broomhandle' remained intact. Of course, they also demanded the prodigious firepower of the famous original. Of all the Spanish guns, the Astra range is the superior, with fit, finish and function comparable with Mauser weapons. Overall sales were respectable, but did not begin to approach those of Mauser. Fewer than 35,000 Astra M900-series pistols were produced, which was a fraction of the roughly one million German-made guns. The majority of the Spanish pistols were sold to their intended market, China. Sales by both companies were routed via Japanese importers, and in the case of Unceta guns were marked in Japanese (either with 'made in Japan' or 'made in the sun country'). Discreet packaging was used to avoid detection, marked euphemistically in English as 'hardware'. Perhaps ironically, a German agent was engaged to facilitate Far Eastern sales.

As mentioned earlier, in a move that must have upset Mauser, after the Spanish Civil War the victorious Nationalist government agreed to sell 'Broomhandle'-pattern pistols to the country that originated them. As in World War I, the rapidly growing German military needed sidearms, but its indigenous gunmakers were at full production capacity. This included Mauser, which had been obliged to cease production of its own M1930

The 20-shot Astra M902. The holster-stock has a special leather 'boot' to accommodate the extended magazine. (© Royal Armouries PR.10737)

The ultimate Astra: the Model F machine pistol, with grip panel unscrewed to show the rate-reducing gear. The typical Astra sideplate is also removed. (© Royal Armouries PR.7534)

and M712 Schnellfeuer in order to concentrate efforts on the P08 'Luger'. An initial order of 1,004 M903 pistols was followed in 1943 by another 2,000 pistols of assorted models.

Although never issued to Spanish government soldiers, the Spanish Mauser copies and derivatives were purchased by military officers. Like their foreign counterparts, they also purchased Mauser originals. Both saw use in the Rif War in Morocco in the early 1920s, a conflict parallel to Britain's earlier colonial wars. Perceived military failures in this war contributed to the military coup of 1926 which in turn led to the Spanish Civil War. As a result, all of the various Mauser-pattern pistols were used in anger within the borders of Spain itself by both the Republican and Nationalist sides. The former seized the remaining guns at the Unceta y Cía factory in Guernica in 1936, while the Nationalists restarted the production lines when they took control of the factory the following year. M900-series pistols were used across the different unit types involved, from regulars to colonial troops, to the various guerrilla fighters with which the conflict is associated. As elsewhere, C96-pattern handguns became somewhat iconic and were brandished for the cameras more than once. Ernest Hemingway incorporated 'long-barrelled' Mausers into his famous novel *For Whom the Bell Tolls* (1940) and his only play, written on the same subject and entitled *The Fifth Column* (1938).

THE MAUSER MYTH

Clearly, the C96 is a technically significant design. It was the first practical self-loading pistol, and its very existence in the market blazed a trail not just for other modern pistols, but for self-loading firearms in general. As with all weapons, however, some of this reputation was owed to elements of folklore and marketing hype. Manufacturers such as Colt were able to elicit glowing testimonials from their large military contracts. By contrast, Mauser and its retailers tended to focus upon the starkly modern appearance and impressive vital statistics of the new technological marvel. Certainly, the high-capacity, self-loading C96 and its high-velocity ammunition compared favourably with clunky and inaccurate European double-action revolvers and slower-firing American favourites like the Colt Single Action Army. With rivals like this in mind, US distributors Von Lengerke & Detmold of New York City advertised with the slogan 'Buy a MAUSER and don't be handicapped' (Anon 1901: 200). Professional and even conscript militaries may have been reluctant to embrace the C96 officially, but in the media and the popular imagination, the C96 was a death-dealing wonder weapon. In 1899, *Scientific American* called it 'the most deadly weapon of its kind ever invented ... practically as good in the hands of marksmen as a Krag-Jorgensen, a Lee, or a Mauser rifle' (Anon 1899c: 210). The writer of a letter to the *Chicago Chronicle* newspaper in 1900 actually bemoaned its mechanical killing efficiency, complaining that it 'doesn't resemble a firearm at all, but looks like some strange scientific instrument'. (Anon 1900: 2) Comments like these were widely published in newspapers around the world.

The world of fiction also enthused, although in a sign of things to come the C96 sometimes appeared as the weapon of a hitman or other criminal. Early 'true crime' writer H. Ashton-Wolfe claimed that 'La Science', a member of the infamous French 'Bonnot Gang', carried four Mausers in his jacket pockets, among other weapons and explosives. The Mausers in this case, however, were a figment of the author's imagination. Journalist Emily Soldene reported in 1899 on her husband's purchase of a C96, and the 'intense' interest that it generated, calling it 'a formidable looking thing, holding ten men's lives' (Soldene 1899: 7). None other than Sir Arthur Conan Doyle referred to the weapon as a 'black, long-barrelled, wicked-looking pistol' in his short story 'One Crowded Hour', published in various newspapers and periodicals in 1911 and reprinted in the collection *Danger! And Other Stories* (Doyle 2007: 53). Of course, by this later date the Mauser had been cemented in its role as a weapon of the enemy; of Germany. This kind of myth-making was essentially free marketing for Mauser, and no doubt influenced many commercial sales as well as private military purchasers like those quoted above. It was (and remains) a dramatic weapon to behold, its rapid fire generating an impressive amount of noise, flash, sparks and flying cartridge cases for such a small weapon.

TURNING TO THE DARK SIDE

Perhaps inevitably given the ready availability of pistols at this time, and the capability of the C96 both real and imagined, quantities of these desirable high-tech pistols did fall into criminal hands. As a result, rather like the AR-15 'black rifle' of today, the 'Broomhandle' gained a partly negative reputation that even prompted debates over gun control. Unlawful use of the C96 was not limited to the pages of lurid novels or early movies, however. In *The Half-Deck*, the sailor George H. Grant wrote autobiographically of an attempted mutiny by Chinese firemen on a British steamer in the Atlantic Ocean in the early years of the 20th century: 'With all my might I swung my handspike. The Chinaman with the Mauser pistol glanced around, strove to dodge, but the bar, whistling through the air, crashed into his face and he went down like a stone into the scupper' (Grant 1935: 270).

Contemporary newspaper reports reveal numerous incidents 'starring' Mauser pistols, notably wherever law enforcement caught up with armed criminals. In the summer of 1903 a unit of 12 Carabinieri ran down the locally infamous Mazzone brothers, cornering them in a cave on the Karsa estate in San Mauro Castelverde, Italy. The two men were able to put up a rugged defence lasting two hours, using single-shot Vetterli rifles and their Mauser pistols to fend off the attackers and wound several of them. Eventually the brothers succumbed to superior numbers, no doubt having run low on ammunition, and were shot dead. On 28 August 1912, at Szakowa in Galicia, another two 'bandits' (apparently Russians) exchanged 400 rounds with Austrian police. The media made sure to highlight the 'enormous number of shots' fired at the police by the criminal identified as Mielenk from the 'Mauser repeater hidden under his overcoat' (Anon 1912: 1).

In September 1914 the infamous Foster Gang of armed robbers took refuge in a cave near Johannesburg. There was no great shootout with South African police, however, as John Maxim, Carl Meza and ringleader William Foster opted instead to take their own lives using the tools of their criminal trade. Tragically, Foster's wife had agreed to visit him in the cave, and she too died, either at her own hand or Foster's. Two C96 pistols and a quantity of ammunition were found next to the bodies. Another four men who committed a series of armed robberies in Warsaw in January 1911 were reported as being armed with Mauser pistols without even being apprehended. This is likely because the C96 was one of the only handguns distinctive enough to be identified by a non-expert eyewitness.

Infamous German murderer Ernst Wagner used two C96 pistols in his September 1913 killing spree in the town of Mühlhausen an der Enz. The firepower offered by these weapons was a threat for which contemporary law enforcement was ill-prepared. Two pistols with ten rounds apiece might allow a shooter to keep one weapon ready to fire at all times. Fortunately, Wagner failed to reload and was overcome by locals, beaten unconscious and arrested, but not before the former schoolteacher was able to kill more than a dozen people. In this period, however, petty criminals and murderers with guns were perceived as a much lesser threat to public order than the activities of militant political movements like the Bolshevists and the anarchists. These people too would become connected with the 'Broomhandle', which as a result would become celebrated and vilified in equal measure.

Shortly before World War I, a number of armed foreign anarchists were active in London, and the C96 became associated with this criminal element, rather like the Thompson submachine gun of the archetypal Chicago gangster. In 1909, a policeman was murdered by anarchists armed with modern self-loading pistols (not Mausers) in what became known as the 'Tottenham Outrage'. In December 1910, four so-called 'Russians' carrying Mauser and Dreyse pistols shot dead three policemen; the greatest single loss of life in British police history. Ringleader George Gardstein carried a C96 in a specially made trouser pocket concealment – no mean feat given the bulk of the weapon. Two members of the same criminal gang went on to fight a protracted street battle with police at 100 Sidney Street the following January. It was rumoured that the renowned Latvian anarchist 'Peter the Painter' was one of the gunmen. 'Peter' was a semi-mythical figure originally named as a 'Peter Piatkow', latterly identified as Janis Zhaklis (a sometime painter and decorator, hence the nickname). The gang's choice of Mauser pistols and the resulting firepower

What's in a name?

The Mauser 'Broomhandle' has received more than its fair share of names, nicknames and designations. This is perhaps because it was never given one official name. Even the Mauser company itself was inconsistent with its official nomenclature, using a variety of long-form descriptive names in preference to snappy model designations and irrespective of many design changes. The only consistent name from inception to the close of production was 'Pistole 7,63' or 'P-7,63' for the original chambering. Other official names were 'Armeepistole', 'Rücklauf-Pistole System Mauser' (1896), 'Selbstlader-Pistole', 'Striefenlader', (late 19th–early 20th centuries), and latterly the specific terms 'Zehnlader-Pistole' and 'Schnellfeuer-Pistole', and the generic 'Rückstoßladepistole' (1930s). All of these were typically prefixed with the Mauser name and suffixed with the calibre (e.g. 'Mauser-Selbstlader-Pistole, Kaliber 7,63 mm'). Of the model designations, only 'C96', 'M96', 'M712' (the Schnellfeuer) and 'M1930' seem to have ever been officially applied ('M' standing for the German 'Modell'). Even 'C96', its most common name today, was rarely used until the mid-20th century. It appears (in the form 'C/96') in the official Mauser history (1938) and seems to be an unofficial shorthand for 'design of 1896'. All other model designations, such as 'M711', 'M713', 'Model 1902', 'Model 1912' and 'M1932', were conceived after World War II along with various nicknames as attempts to classify the many subtle variations on the type. The same is true of the purely descriptive 'Red Nine' (or 'Rot Neun'). Even the famous 'Broomhandle' (often 'Broomhandle Mauser') nickname, which has gained widespread popular recognition, was not contemporaneous with the production of the weapon itself. The first written usage of 'Broomhandle' is a 1966 classified advertisement in a US magazine. The word *Kuhfuß* meaning 'crowbar' (literally 'cow's foot') has also been suggested as a soldier's nickname for the C96; but despite long-standing German military usage to describe ungainly muskets and rifles, there is no hard evidence that it was used for pistols. The Chinese name *hezi pao* (盒子炮) or 'Box Cannon', is a play on the large size and wooden case of the C96 in current use, and may also have seen period usage. As for the term 'Bolo', this was indeed period British slang for 'Bolshevik'; the 'Bolos' certainly did use C96s, and the short-barrelled variant was the main variant produced by Mauser throughout the period in question. Written evidence is again lacking, however. By this measure, the best-attested C96 nickname by far is the Irish 'Peter the Painter'.

'overmatch' suffered by the London police was widely reported. The incident became popularly known as 'The Siege of Sidney Street' or 'The Battle of Stepney'. The situation was serious enough that then-Home Secretary Winston Churchill attended the scene. One senior police officer received a bullet through his hat brim. In the end, the siege was broken by rifle-armed soldiers of The Scots Guards, who fired some 500 rounds in the effort. A Maxim machine gun and two QF 13-pdr artillery pieces were eventually brought up, but were not required.

The authorities faced stiff criticism in the press about the handling of the incident, and much was made in their defence of the threat posed by the Mauser pistol with its greater accuracy, rate of fire and range compared with other handguns. Pro-police newspapers even dubbed the weapons 'miniature Gatling guns' and 'grim messengers of death' (Anon 1911: 5). When the shooting finally stopped and the area was searched two bodies were found along with, papers claimed, as many as twelve Mauser pistols (with a belt of 150 'soft-nosed' cartridges) and 'several' Brownings. In reality only two C96s and one 7.65mm FN Browning (either M1900 or M1910) were recovered. Despite this rather modest arsenal, a popular panic ensued: Britain might soon be overrun by nefarious 'aliens' armed with these terrifying weapons. The perceived social and political threat resulted in new proposed legislation to limit the rights of immigrants, including some of the first real efforts at gun control in the UK.

The emphasis placed upon the dreaded Mauser was so strong that Wirt Gerrare, a travel writer and author of *An Encyclopaedia of Guns and Shooting*, attempted to debunk the media claims. Rather than being 'some wondrous magic' as Gerrare summarized the popular misconception, it was in reality 'quite an ordinary type of weapon' (Gerrare 1911: 154). It might be more effective than a normal pistol, but it was inferior to any rifle. He pointed out that people tended to mistake its sighted range of 1,000m as its effective range, and berated newspaper journalists for seeking to instil fear in the public. Gerrare's comments were reproduced in some newspapers, but made little impact. The weapon's reputation and the myth of Sidney Street had already been made. The police of the day, ill-equipped and ill-prepared to respond to determined armed criminals in an urban environment, were happy to let the blame fall on foreign technology and foreign enemies rather than their organizational and political masters. One of the C96s (serial 66,531) recovered from 100 Sidney Street was used as an exhibit in the subsequent court case to emphasize this point. It resides today in the collection of the Metropolitan Police's Crime Museum as a reminder to today's officers of the threat posed by firearms.

The Siege of Sidney Street was used to justify the purchase of modern self-loading pistols for Metropolitan Police officers. Trials were hastily arranged less than two weeks after the siege was brought to a conclusion, the winner being the decidedly British and decidedly underpowered Webley .32, rebranded the 'M.P.' for police issue. The dead anarchists meanwhile were tentatively identified (they had been burned beyond recognition) as Latvians Fritz Svaars and William (aka Josef) Sokolov. Peter the Painter was nowhere to be found. Yet the number and identity of those involved is still uncertain to this day. The real Peter may or may not have been present at Sidney Street (he probably was not), but he too was reputed to favour the Mauser for its penetrative power. In any event, the siege helped to cement the fearsome reputation of the pistol. In 1916, Irish republicans, also facing down British security forces, dubbed their pistols 'Peter the Painter' after this legendary anarchist ringleader.

'PETER THE PAINTER'

Though the C96 was a pioneering early design, its popularity into the 20th century might seem curious at first glance. More modern designs such as the Colt M1911, and more proven pistols in the form of revolvers, were available. Moreover, pistols are not particularly capable weapons, militarily speaking. Even so, in the sporadic street fighting and countryside ambushes that characterized the Easter Rising and indeed later actions, pistols – and the C96 in particular – would take on a disproportionate significance.

The first Irish paramilitary actions against the British Crown took place in 1916 and became known as the 'Easter Rising'. As non-state military forces, the various Irish units involved had no standard-issue arms and were obliged to obtain what they could from overseas. The resulting acquisitions ranged from obsolete single-shot rifles to up-to-date designs such as the Colt M1911. Among the more sought-after weapons was the 'Broomhandle'. Although Germany, as the proverbial 'enemy of my enemy' in 1916, would seem a natural source of arms, in fact little direct military aid was supplied. Even if it had been, it was unlikely that the C96, pressed into military service in Germany that same year, would have made it across the sea in significant numbers. A number of those legally purchased by Irish civilians would already have been available to the rebels, purchased from retailers in Ireland and

Irish Volunteers Jack Doyle and Tom McGrath at the Dublin General Post Office, April 1916. McGrath has a holstered C96 on his belt. (Courtesy of Kilmainham Gaol Museum, KMGLM 2011.0166)

mainland Britain. Given the acquisition (by both sides) of Mauser rifles from a dealer in Hamburg, it also seems likely that pistols were acquired direct from Germany. Both 7.63×25mm and 9×19mm variants saw service, as surviving examples attest. We know from the official history written for the Irish Bureau of Military History that one pistol was sold to a member of the Irish Volunteers by the Irish Republican Army (IRA) for £12, a full £3 more than the price for rifles purchased on the same occasion. Where the rifle was the more powerful, accurate, reliable and long-ranged option and would more usually be the more expensive item, the Mauser was far more wieldy and concealable in an urban environment and already had an iconic image for Irish fighters.

By the time of the pivotal Easter Rising in April 1916, the Mauser pistols had become sought-after status symbols but also practical fighting tools, described as 'formidable weapons' by the *Weekly Irish Times* newspaper (Anon 1917: 132). When Padraig Pearce, leader of the Rising, surrendered on 30 April 1916, the sidearm he turned in was a C96. His second-in-command, Cathal Brugha, used another in the defence of the South Dublin Union building. The celebrated revolutionary figure Countess Markiewicz used a C96 against a British machine-gun position on the roof of the Shelbourne Hotel. This pistol, serial numbered 162742, was handed in to the new Irish government at a ceremony on Friday 29 April 1949. The pistol had been given to Markiewicz by James Connolly, commandant of the Dublin Brigade, the main armed IRA unit active in the Rising. Realizing that she was without her usual revolvers as they prepared to take on British forces, the Countess exclaimed, 'But, Mr Connolly, I haven't my pistol on me.' Connolly replied, 'Never mind, Madame, we'll give you one' (Connolly 1918: 30–31). Markiewicz then insisted that they hand it to her right away for her peace of mind. The Countess used the handgun to attack the British machine-gun crew atop the nearby Shelbourne Hotel. Eventually captured, she surrendered the pistol to British Captain Harry de Courcy-Wheeler, and it is now in the collection of the National Museum of Ireland.

The C96 features in numerous recorded 'old' IRA actions. Perhaps the most infamous incident was the Battle of Mount Street Bridge, the high point of the Rising for the Republican side. In this skirmish, 17 Irish Volunteers were able to account for 240 British casualties. Lieutenant

This C96 belonged to Michael Murphy who supposedly used it in the attack on the Customs House during the War of Independence (25 May 1921). Murphy was later on the Anti-Treaty side of the Civil War and was imprisoned in 1923. While in prison he renounced violence and when released surrendered his weapon to his employer Denis Rourke, a close friend of Michael Davitt, a prominent Republican politician. Rourke in turn passed the gun to Davitt who had it in his possession until he donated it to Kilmainham Gaol in the 1960s. (Courtesy of Kilmainham Gaol Museum, 19HG-2A23-01)

Michael 'Mick' Malone of the Irish Volunteers was stationed at 25 Northumberland Road as part of a small force of 16 men tasked with fortifying the bridge. If the bridge fell, the British would be able to reinforce their existing units inside the city and crush the Rising. Malone had borrowed a Mauser C96 from commandant (later President) Éamon De Valera, and together with another man opened fire on a unit of reservist soldiers that he believed intended to attack. In fact, they were on their way home from manoeuvres with unloaded rifles. The impartial Mauser of course did its work regardless, killing and wounding several men. The actual attack, by men of 1/7th Battalion, The Sherwood Foresters (Nottinghamshire and Derbyshire Regiment), came two days later on 26 April 1916. In the action that ensued Malone, defending a house on the corner of Northumberland Road and Haddington Road, was reportedly able to strike ten soldiers with each of the ten rounds in his weapon. He reloaded repeatedly, firing so many shots that the weapon became too hot to continue fire, and he resorted to his obsolete Mauser Gew 71 single-shot rifle. In these conditions, rapid fire was more important than range, accuracy, or even lethality. Malone and his comrade Seamus Grace were forced to fall back from the barricade that they had built at the front door of the house. Malone was shot dead as he came down the stairs by British soldiers who had entered via the back door. Grace was found alive having reached the relative safety of the basement after his weapon jammed during the desperate gunfight. Inevitably, the far superior numbers of the British force won the day, but a handful of guerrilla fighters had exacted a terrible toll of 216 men and four officers. Four of the Volunteers escaped with their lives, and the British counter-attack was delayed. Around 20 civilians had lost their lives, however, trying to assist the fallen British soldiers.

The C96 saw even more use through the subsequent Irish War of Independence (1919–22) and Irish Civil War (1922–23). Vincent 'Vinny' Byrne was a pistol instructor for the IRA and one of 'Twelve Apostles' in an assassination squad formed by Michael Collins. Among his papers are handwritten notes and sketches on the component parts of the C96, which he too calls 'Peter the Painter'. Given the number of Mauser pistols in Republican hands, it was essential that Byrne and other instructors, armourers and small-arms specialists be familiar with the type.

On 9 July 1921, against the background of a negotiated truce between the British government and Irish Republican party Sinn Féin, an ambush took place on Belfast's Raglan Street. It was a response to an armed raid by Royal Irish Constabulary officers claimed by the IRA to have murderous intent. Despite opposing gunfire from 14 IRA shooters, all three police casualties were the work of one IRA man armed with a C96. Sean Montgomery recalled what happened. 'We turned a corner then a shout in a Southern Brogue, 'Halt, hands up!' Jack Donaghy was using a Peter Painter 12 rounder. He opened fire, three Policemen fell, one killed and two wounded' (National Library of Ireland, Ms 44,061/6). The murder of PC Conlan triggered the infamous 'Bloody Sunday' civil unrest in which a further 16 people (Catholics and Protestants) died. Thus the deadly potential of a Mauser pistol in the right – or wrong – hands played its part in the history of violence in Ireland. It would not be the last time.

No other country seems to have so deliberately memorialized the weapon. The pistols belonging to Pearce, Markiewicz, Malone and Byrne are all now preserved as artefacts of the Easter Rising in the National Museum of Ireland, and more are to be found in other Irish museums. Because of this important if bloody history, 'Peter the Painter' pistols became trophies of the Republican struggle to the later, overtly terrorist evolutions of the IRA. These men often had to rely upon older arms such as the Enfield rifle and Thompson submachine gun. But these were hardly antiques. One Ardoyne volunteer described the large quantities of vintage yet fully functional firearms provided to the Official and Provisional IRA in the 1970s, cached decades earlier or kept hidden in houses.

Stories such as that of Mount Street have cemented the Mauser pistol's place in Irish history. Such is the legend of 'Peter the Painter' that it is often credited with the 1922 assassination of Irish Free State commander Michael Collins by elements of the IRA of which he had formerly been a part. Many in the IRA saw Collins as a traitor to the Republican cause. There are also suggestions that a member of Collins' own bodyguard, who carried a C96, might have been the killer. The claim that a Mauser pistol was used is made on the basis that only the legendary 'Peter the Painter', and not a rifle bullet, could have inflicted Collins' devastating head wound. This is absolutely backwards; any rifle would readily produce such a wound, while a pistol like the C96 would very likely not. There is no bullet, no murder weapon, and no other evidence to go on, save for an horrific head wound with a small entry hole. In the absence of a suspect in the case, 'Peter' seems to have made a convenient mechanical scapegoat, symbolizing the fractured nature of the Republican movement and of Ireland during the Irish Civil War. It would indeed be an ironic moral to the story if a weapon so identified with the Republican cause and one used to protect Collins turned out to be his undoing. Even so, whatever really happened that day, it is unlikely that 'Peter' was turned on his former master in this way.

Yet the Mauser did gain a reputation as an assassin's weapon, in part because of Yermakov's political murder of the Russian Empress Alexandra in July 1918 (see page 25). But 'Comrade Mauser' was not the only high-profile murderer to favour the C96. All of the same attributes that gave the design such potential for legitimate users were as much a boon to criminals. In one 1909 newspaper article bemoaning the use of modern handguns by assassins, the Mauser pistol was the only weapon mentioned by name. Given the availability of pocket revolvers since the mid-19th century, this might seem strange. In part it reflects the high media profile and intimidating looks of the C96, but there was some practical truth to the matter. The 'Broomhandle' may have been large and hefty, but it was also slimmer, quicker to fire and carried twice as many shots as many small revolvers. Ten (or even 20) rapid shots would increase the chance of hitting someone, and if they were hit, of mortally wounding them.

Only two years after the introduction of the Mauser Schnellfeuer, it was made infamous in the assassination of Alexander Karadjordjevic, King Alexander I of Yugoslavia. Alexander was targeted by Vlado Chernozemski of the Internal Macedonian Revolutionary Organization as the king's car drove through Marseille on 9 October 1934. Chernozemski jumped onto the vehicle's running board with his pistol concealed in a bunch of flowers. At such close range, he could not miss, and the king, the French foreign minister Louis Barthou who was riding next to him, and their chauffeur were all mortally wounded (the king dying at the scene). The assassin then exchanged fire with the king's bodyguards, resulting in another 14 people being wounded. As he attempted to escape, Chernozemski was cut down by Colonel Jules Piolet, the officer commanding the French honour guard, using his sabre. The assassination was actually captured on film, though neither Chernozemski nor the murder weapon can be seen. The Schnellfeuer pistol used to such deadly effect by Chernozemski was retained by the authorities and remains on display in the Belgrade Military Museum.

As practically effective as the C96 could be, the mythology and cultural impact of the type cannot be overstated. As we have seen from the Chinese and Irish experiences, it was as much a symbol of personal firepower as a weapon. It saw use in both ways in countless conflicts, including the oppression visited upon Armenian civilians by the Ottoman Empire in 1914–15, often known as the 'Armenian Genocide'. As in China, it seems that pistols were preferred. The British Consul reported that the Mauser was 'easier to import and could be hidden on one's person' (Kaligian 2011: 216). This is true of all pistols, of course, but the C96 in particular was, in the words of political scientist Arus Harutyunyan, 'an Armenian weapon of choice in the close hand-to-hand fighting within the city of Van itself' (Harutyunyan 2009: 85). One powerful example of this is a photograph (see page 1) taken during the Armenian Genocide that shows an armed civil-defence group not unlike those formed today in Mexico in response to the violence visited by the drugs cartels. They wear a mixture of contemporary suits and traditional Armenian dress. All but one proudly display their Mauser pistols with loaded chargers inserted in an added show of force and potential firepower. Two hold up homemade signs for the camera that read 'ASHKHATANK' meaning 'work', the name of a communist periodical and part of a socialist slogan ('Hairenik, Ashkhatank, Sotsializm' or 'Fatherland, Work, Socialism').

The C96 had also become iconic in Iran by the 1910s. British officer Lionel C. Dunsterville reported that a local official thought to be collaborating with the British was sent a death threat. At the head of the

Members of the Shanghai Municipal Police demonstrate the ballistic vest. It is believed that the vest was designed to be 'Mauser proof'. (Dorothea Fairbairn/Leroy Thompson)

letter was a drawing of a Mauser pistol in threatening red ink. Even in post-World War I Germany, where the C96 had acted as a substitute to the standard issue P08 'Luger', the weapon could still serve as a symbol of defiance to those resisting the demilitarization of the country. Freikorps officer Rudolf Mann mistakenly conflated the two weapons in his 1921 propaganda book *Mit Ehrhardt durch Deutschland*: 'Innumerable newspapers reported for the benefit of history that the sword had been struck out of the traitors' hands. The sword was a 0,8 Mauser pistol [*sic*], but I have that still, and so have my comrades. No one struck that out of our hands' (quoted in Anon 1921: 3).

In China, part of the legendary status of the 'Box Cannon' included its reputation as a criminal weapon. Notably, the internationally settled urban area of Shanghai had become a dangerous place in the 1920s and 1930s, described in the press as a 'pistol-ridden city' (Anon 1929: 2). Some of the many violent criminals operating there were ex-soldiers who had brought their 7.63mm service pistols with them. This level of popular concern resulted in the retraining and re-equipping of the local Shanghai Municipal Police (SMP) under the influence of British martial artists and gunfighters William Fairbairn and Eric Sykes, who would go on to train

'Broomhandle' v2.0: the Type 80 machine pistol. Chinese designers tried to keep the spirit of the Mauser alive in the form of the Type 80, developed in the late 1970s for paratroopers and officers not requiring a full-sized rifle. While being a largely novel design, this weapon preserved the silhouette of the Mauser, together with the detachable wooden holster-stock. It chambered the same cartridge, although it was designed to withstand the higher pressures of the Russian 7.62×25mm Tokarev loading. Moreover, the barrel and front portion of the barrel extension were directly based upon the M1930/M712. Ultimately, the Type 80 was never issued and only a few thousand were produced. (Courtesy of Yuan Wei)

special-operations forces and spies in World War II. Fear of criminals armed with Mauser-pattern pistols was not limited to the public or authorities, however.

The 7.63mm bullet was a genuine concern for policemen obliged to assault armed criminals in difficult urban situations. Even among the brave and experienced men of the SMP, it was reported by Fairbairn & Sykes that 'nothing is so feared, rightly or wrongly, as the Mauser military automatic. The mention of the word is sufficient, if there is trouble afoot, to send men in instant search of bullet-proof equipment' (Fairbairn & Sykes 1987: 75). Indeed, by 1928 Fairbairn had developed (and had issued) ballistic vests for the SMP entry teams. Metal laths were fashioned into protective panels covering breast, back, side, groin and even the tops of the shoulders. These were then secured into fabric covers, the complete vest weighing nearly 10kg. Special effort was devoted to a heavy (12.2kg) 'Mauser-Proof' version. Early forms of mobile ballistic entry shield (the heavier of which weighed 18kg) were also devised to give the men the necessary protection and confidence to take on wielders of the formidable 'Box Cannon'.

A STAR OF THE SILVER SCREEN

Few today would recognize the fearsome historical reputation of the C96 or even think of it as Conan Doyle did, as 'wicked-looking' (Doyle 2007: 53). In fact, few would know its correct designation or even much of its history – but they would very likely recognize its lines and, like previous generations, something of its mythical status. The pistol's distinctive, bulky, purposeful shape proved a popular choice in film and television. Its best-known role is as the 'blaster' used by Han Solo and Luke Skywalker in the original Star Wars film trilogy, bearing the fictional designation of 'DL-44'. It is safe to say that many are now more familiar with the C96 in this movie role than as an historical firearm. Like other vintage types adapted by propmasters Bapty & Co., the C96 was 'dressed up' to create a realistic-looking workaday weapon, with energy blasts to be animated in post-production.

In reality, Solo's blaster is part of a cinematic tradition of 'casting' distinctive-looking firearms in a prominent role. The Mauser prop was originally conceived as a take-down sniping rifle for an unsuccessful Frank Sinatra thriller called *The Naked Runner* (1967). A telescopic sight was mounted to the left side, and the barrel was cut off and replaced with a short, heavy, threaded unit onto which a long rifle barrel could be screwed. For the Star Wars films, another C96 with the same barrel arrangement was fitted instead with a silver machine-gun flash suppressor, and the 'scope was moved to the right side in order to fit a holster. To break up the recognisable lines of the Mauser, several model-kit parts were attached. The large flat C96 offered plenty of surfaces on which to attach disguising parts, but the weapon remains unmistakable despite these additions. Director George Lucas wanted his 'space guns' to look familiar and realistic, but still other-worldly in appearance.

The Lone Star 'Man From U.N.C.L.E.' cap-gun toy. (Courtesy of King Rhoton)

Other notable movie roles include Churchill's sidearm in *Young Winston*, and in the Clint Eastwood western *Joe Kidd* (both 1972). The latter movie (set a few years after the C96's debut) nicely reflects period attitudes to the new high-tech pistol, as Eastwood easily bests his revolver-armed foes. In *The Rocketeer* (1991), the choice is a stylistic one, the weapon's lines complementing the Futurist/Art Deco stylings of the main character. With shades of the retro-futuristic 'Steampunk' movement (within which it is a perennial favourite), the M712 Schnellfeuer featured as a plausibly Victorian machine pistol in Guy Ritchie's *Sherlock Holmes: A Game of Shadows* (2011). The C96, too, made a deliberately anachronistic appearance in the gothic-horror TV series *Penny Dreadful* (2014). It proves to be an effective slayer of vampires and witches, but there is real history underlying this choice. Timothy Dalton's Sir Malcolm Murray character is an explorer and hunter, making his interest in modern firearms and the C96 in particular quite appropriate. A genuine cased antique 'conehammer' was carefully chosen to serve as a 'prototype'. In both cases (these productions are both set in the early 1890s) the message to the viewer is clear: this was a weapon ahead of its time, an elegant icon of destruction, as impressive to modern audiences as it would have been to the Victorians.

The type has also proven to be a popular model for children's toys. Toy company Lone Star produced a 'Young Mr. Churchill: War Correspondent' cap gun in the 1960s, reusing the same dies for another toy licensed to TV spy thriller *The Man From U.N.C.L.E.* This was no doubt a money-saving effort, given that the famous pistol with stock and silencer in that TV show was the quite different Walther P38. This cultural rehabilitation of the 'Broomhandle' is fascinating. Prior to the 1970s, it had (along with the P08 'Luger' and Walther P38) become an archetypal 'bad guy' gun, with high-profile usage by the German militaries (including the Nazis), warriors of the mysterious 'Orient', Bolshevist revolutionaries, insurgents, anarchists, terrorists and common criminals. Today it is an icon of advanced Victorian technology and the spirit of adventure, more likely to appear in the hands of a plucky hero than those of a moustache-twirling villain. Finally, of course, it is also studied and admired by legions of collectors, enthusiasts and other students of history.

CONCLUSION

The 'Broomhandle' was not the first self-loading pistol, nor the first machine pistol. It wasn't even the first such weapon to see military adoption. From a technical point of view its various mechanisms failed to set any real trend, later successful designs following the external 'slide' approach popularized by the FN and Colt designs of John Browning. Overall, it has to be said that the C96 pales in comparison with later pistol designs and would be unsuitable for today's various military, police and civilian needs. Nevertheless, it must be remembered that in 1896 there was simply nothing in its class to touch its firepower, reliability and accuracy potential. It is often said that the Borchardt was the first successful self-loading pistol, but in reality that accolade should fall to the Mauser-designed 'Broomhandle'. It amassed around one million sales in 40 years of production, whereas the Borchardt reached only a few thousand. This places the Mauser on a par with much more developed designs like the Walther P38 and Browning Hi-Power, though far behind leaders like the P08 'Luger', Colt M1911 and Makarov PM. At a time when most handguns were limited to six shots, the Mauser caught the attention of the world with its unprecedented firepower and powerful high-velocity cartridge. In this sense, the Mauser holds a place in history as a trailblazer for modern pistols.

Importantly, Mauser's design was also the first to see actual combat, arming both sides in the Second Anglo-Boer War. The compact firepower embodied in the 'Broomhandle' saw its ultimate expression in the various selective-fire designs that followed, Mauser's M712 Schnellfeuer being the most popular. Dedicated long-barrelled 'hunting' and 'trench' carbines may have been rendered redundant by the shoulder stock of the standard variants, but the latter configuration foreshadowed the compact submachine gun or 'Personal Defence Weapon' of today. Though official military take-up was limited, the C96, its copies and derivatives saw military, paramilitary or police service with the forces of at least 19 countries, including Austria, Brazil, Bolivia, Britain, China, the Dutch East Indies, Finland, Hungary, Ireland, Israel, Italy, Persia, Russia, Singapore, South Africa, Spain, Turkey, the United States, and of course its home country of Germany. Widely purchased commercially, the 'Broomhandle' gained a fearsome reputation on both sides of the law, became Winston Churchill's favourite weapon, and passed into legend thanks to its paramilitary usage. The infamous 'Peter the Painter' grew larger than any tangible impact that the Mauser (or any pistol for that matter) could have had in reality. This piece of 19th-century technology has even made it into space, albeit only in our collective imagination. Thus, although long out of production and with its service history now well behind it, the C96 has already been immortalized in fiction and is likely to remain a staple of books, films and video games for decades to come. In fact, those without firearms knowledge are far more likely to recognize the type in its dressed-up movie-prop guise than as a piece of real history. Not as famous as the P08 'Luger', as influential as the Walther P38, nor as stalwart in service as the Colt M1911, the Mauser C96 nevertheless has an important place in firearms history and remains an iconic and distinctive design today.

The definitive production 'conehammer' Mauser pistol, this example manufactured in 1897. (© Royal Armouries PR.11417)

GLOSSARY

BOLT	The metal block that, together with the cartridge case, seals the **CHAMBER** against the high-pressure gas released to propel the bullet.
CHAMBER	The rearmost portion of a firearm's barrel, which supports the cartridge for firing and, together with the breech or **BOLT**, contains the resulting high-pressure gas.
CHARGER	Aka 'stripper clip'. A feed device without a spring, designed to hold cartridges for feeding into the **MAGAZINE** or **CHAMBER** of a firearm.
DISCONNECTOR	Mechanical device that disconnects the trigger from the **SEAR**, primarily to limit a pistol to semi-automatic fire.
DOUBLE ACTION	A type of trigger mechanism in which the **HAMMER** is not only released but also cocked by a single long pull of the trigger. The 'Broomhandle' family are all 'single action' only.
EXTRACTOR	The part, usually a small metal hook, that removes a spent cartridge case from the **CHAMBER** after firing.
FIELD STRIP	The minimal disassembly of a firearm for cleaning and maintenance.
HAMMER	The part of a pistol that is released (by means of a **SEAR**) by pulling the trigger, falling forward under spring tension to strike the firing pin.
MAGAZINE	A feed device with integral spring, designed to hold cartridges for feeding into the **CHAMBER** of a firearm.
MAGAZINE FOLLOWER	The sprung platform in a **MAGAZINE** that positions cartridges for feeding.
SAFETY CATCH	Aka 'safety'. A mechanism designed to prevent inadvertent discharge of a firearm.
SEAR	Part of the trigger mechanism that translates movement from the trigger to the **HAMMER**.
SELECTIVE-FIRE	A self-loading weapon that may be fired in semi-automatic or automatic modes by means of a selector control.

BIBLIOGRAPHY

Published sources

Anonymous (1899a). 'Rifles, Revolvers, & Pistols', in *Country Life Illustrated*, 4 March 1899: 264.

Anonymous (1899b). 'Wicked-looking weapon', in *Indianapolis Journal*, Vol. 49, No. 290, 17 October 1899: 4.

Anonymous (1899c). 'The Mauser Pistol', in *Scientific American*, 30 September 1899: 210.

Anonymous (1900). *The Citizen*, 28 February 1900: 2.

Anonymous (1901). 'An American Officer's Observations', in *Shooting & Fishing*, Vol. 30, No. 12, July 1901: 225–26.

Anonymous (1911). 'One Thousand to Two', in *West Gippsland Gazette*, 21 March 1911: 5.

Anonymous (1912). 'A Pistol Duel', in *The Evening Star*, 28 August 1912: 1.

Anonymous (1916). *The Straits Times*, 17 January 1916: 8.

Anonymous (1917). *Sinn Fein Rebellion Handbook, Easter, 1916*. Dublin: The Weekly Irish Times.

Anonymous (1921). 'Adventures in Arms', in *The Northern Advocate*. 3 July 1921: 3.

Anonymous (1929). 'A Brave Detective', in *The Northern Miner*. 27 August 1929: 2.

Antaris, Leonardo M. (1988). *Astra Automatic Pistols*. Sterling, CO: FIRAC.

Baudino, Mauro & van Vlimmeren, Gerben (2017). *Paul Mauser: His Life, Company, and Handgun Development 1838–1914*. Galesburg, IL: Brad Simpson.

Belford, James N. & Dunlap, Jack (1969). *The Mauser Self-Loading Pistol*. Alhambra, CA: Borden.

Bell, W.D.M. (1923). *The Wanderings of an Elephant Hunter*. London: Scribner.

Breathed, Jr, John W. & Schroeder, Joseph J. (1967). *System Mauser: A Pictorial History of the Model 1896 Self-Loading Pistol*. Glenview, IL: Handgun Press.

Cadogan, W.G. (1908). 'The Wreck of the "Ismore"', in *The 10th Royal Hussars Gazette*. Vol. 1 No. 4, July 1908: 54–55.

Churchill, Winston S. (1902). *The River War by Sir Winston Churchill*. Vol. 2. London: Longmans.

Churchill, Winston S. (1930). *A Roving Commission: My Early Life*. New York, NY: Scribner.

Coleman, Frederic (1916). *From Mons to Ypres with French: A Personal Narrative*. Toronto: Briggs.

Connolly, Nora (1918). *The Unbroken Tradition*. New York, NY: Boni & Liveright.

Doyle, A.C. (2007). 'One Crowded Hour', in *Danger! And Other Stories*. Project Gutenberg edition, 50-71. Originally published in 1918.

Dunsterville, L.C. (1920). *The Adventures of Dunsterforce*. London: Edward Arnold.

Erickson, Wayne R. & Pate, Charles (1985). *Broomhandle Pistol, 1896–1936*. Toronto: Collector Grade.

Fairbairn, William Ewart & Sykes, Eric Anthony (1987). *Shooting to Live*. Boulder, CO: Paladin. First published in 1942.

Fraser, D. (1910). *Persia and Turkey in Revolt*. Edinburgh: Blackwood.

Garnett, David, ed. (1939). *The Letters of T.E. Lawrence*. New York, NY: Doubleday.

Gerrare, Wirt (1911). 'The Mauser Fiction', in *Travel and Exploration*. Vol. 5 No. 26, February 1911: 154–55.

Gore, St. John (1901). *The Green Horse in Ladysmith*. London: Sampson Low.

Grant, George H. (1935). *The Half Deck*. London: Hurst.

Kaligian, D.M. (2011). *Armenian Organization and Ideology under Ottoman Rule: 1908–1914*. Piscataway, NJ: Transaction.

Kersten, Manfred, Moll, F.W. & Schmid, Walter (2014). *Mauser C96*. Kleve: Service K.

Manchester, William (1984). *The Last Lion: Winston Spencer Churchill: Visions of Glory, 1874–1932*. New York, NY: Dell.

Maze, Robert J. (2002). *Howdah to High Power: A Century of Breechloading Service Pistols (1867–1967)*. Tucson, AZ: Excalibur Publications.

Skennerton, Ian (2005). *Mauser Model 1896 Pistol Handbook*. Gold Coast: Arms & Militaria Press.

Soldane, Emily (1899). 'London Week by Week', in *The Evening News* (Sydney), 13 December 1899: 7.

Weaver, W. Darin, Speed, Jon & Schmid, Walter (2008). *Mauser Pistolen Development and Production 1877–1945*. Toronto: Collector Grade.

Wilson, H.W. (1900). *With the Flag to Pretoria: A History of the Boer War of 1899–1900, Vol. 1*. London: Harmsworth Bros.

Other sources

Harutyunyan, Arus (2009). 'Contesting National Identities in an Ethnically Homogenous State: the Case of Armenian Democratization.' *Doctoral thesis*. Available at http://scholarworks. wmich.edu/dissertations/667 (accessed 5 April 2017).

IWM Sound Archive 23151.

MoD Pattern Room archive, SAC Minute No. 592/17.2.1902. WO Paper 7101/B/6401.

MoD Pattern Room archive, SAC DGO. 7.5.1902, forwarded WO Paper 7101/B/6582A.

MoD Pattern Room archive, SAC Minute No. 462/WO Paper 7101/B/5733.

MoD Pattern Room Archive, 'Reports on Equipment in S. Africa'.

National Library of Ireland, Ms 44,061/6.

INDEX